Kids,
Alcohol &
Drugs

Kids,
Alcohol &
Drugs

A PARENT'S GUIDE

Ruth Maxwell

BALLANTINE BOOKS
NEW YORK

Copyright © 1991 by Ruth Maxwell

All rights reserved under International and Pan-American Copyright Conventions. Published in the United States by Ballantine Books, a division of Random House, Inc., New York, and simultaneously in Canada by Random House of Canada Limited, Toronto.

Library of Congress Catalog Card Number: 91-91886

ISBN: 0-345-31957-9

Cover design by Kristine V. Mills
Designed by Ann Gold
Manufactured in the United States of America
First Edition: September 1991
10 9 8 7 6 5 4 3 2 1

This book is dedicated to all parents called upon to take extraordinary action with children who developed harmful involvements with chemicals, especially Jackie, Betty and Rich, Carol and Harvey, Phyllis and David, Arlene, Michelle and Dan, Mary Jane and Steve, Marcia and David, Joan, Paula and Jim, Rhoda and Steve, Johanna and Lehn, Peggy and Joe, Fran, Catherine, Francine and Fred, Connie and Allan, Renata, Ginny and Kevin, Penny and Nick, Christine, Sheila and Irving, Natalie and Herb, Carol and Jim, Marilyn, Bernie, Tina and James, Shirley, Angela and Marvin, Marie and Dave, Lenore and Gene, Betty and Paul, Jeanmarie and Mike.

ACKNOWLEDGMENTS

I am grateful to Florence Korzinski, Carol Raff, and Arlene Feltenstein for reading the manuscript in its various stages and for their recommendations and encouraging words. Special thanks to Caroline Whiting for her research, ideas, and assistance when I was about ready to throw in the towel. I am indebted to my editors Joëlle Delbourgo and Elizabeth Zack for their incredible patience and guidance given so kindly. Gratitude goes to my children, Judi, Rachel, and Dan, and to my new son, Edward Poller, for being. And a great big thank you to HP.

CONTENTS

The Kids   xi

Introduction   3

1. The Nature of Adolescence   12

2. Peer Groups   24

3. The Choices Kids Must Make in Today's World   34

4. Why Kids Use Alcohol and Other Drugs   44

5. Drugs of Choice   60

6. Behavior/Personality Changes Associated with Adolescent Chemical Dependency   77

7. Signs of Alcohol and Other Drug Use   89

8. Connecting Chemical Use to Behavior/Personality Changes   104

9. How to Determine Treatment Needs   120

10. Parental Codependency   132

11. How to Help Kids Who Agree to Cooperate   144

12. How to Help Kids Who Are Unwilling to Cooperate: The Structured Intervention   164

13. Kids and Parents in Recovery   188

14. Preventive Parenting   201

Appendices   217

Bibliography   221

Index   224

THE KIDS

TONI experimented with alcohol and marijuana, but her mom nipped her chemical use in the bud. A healthy teenager from a divorced family, Toni faced her share of problems but got the help she needed, so that addiction did not become one of them.

BRIAN, believing he was "too short, too dumb, and way behind everyone," bought friends by supplying them with booze. After finding a stash of pot, his father enforced stricter household rules, and Brian had to find other ways to gain peer approval.

RICKY used heroin to stay connected to his peers. Unable to take a stand and stick to it, his parents could no more let go of Ricky than Ricky could let go of heroin; they all suffered the most dire of consequences.

ALLISON started drinking alcohol in fifth grade, manifesting problems that confused everyone. Perhaps one of the most normal kids in this book from one of the healthiest families, Allison still developed a harmful chemical involvement and needed treatment—which she didn't want but got anyway.

BRAD, a born thrill seeker, was nearly destroyed by chemicals. After stays in three psychiatric hospitals, one school for emotionally disturbed adolescents, innumerable chemical dependency treatment centers and halfway houses, Brad finally got his act together. But first, his parents had to let go.

MARK, an outdoor enthusiast and natural athlete, was devastated by pot. While he worked hard to achieve recovery, getting treatment was actually an easy matter for him. Unlike the other addicted children, Mark readily admitted his problem.

KIMBERLY was a good kid who got the worst possible breaks in life. Deserted by both of her addicted parents, Kimberly joined the drug-using crowd, started using crack, and supported herself and her habit by hooking.

DAVID, cool as they come, hid his addiction well. He denied using, denied problems, and denied needing treatment. Unable to keep the promise he made to his parents, he was treated anyway.

JOANN drank "just like everyone else," according to her dad, but her diary revealed otherwise. Although she eventually got the treatment she needed, thanks to her parents, she nevertheless paid an unthinkable price for her addiction.

TIM'S parents did an intervention, broke through his recalcitrance, and got him to seek treatment. Had they known better, they would have intervened earlier, when Tim's chances for recovery were greater.

Kids,
Alcohol &
Drugs

Introduction

As parents most of us are not crazy, stupid, or incompetent. But our children's use of alcohol or other drugs can make us believe we are.

Some of us do not realize our children are using alcohol or other drugs. We may see behavior in our children that is worrisome, even out of control, but we do not know the reason for it. We go out of our way to make things better—we may even haul our children off for psychotherapy—but our children only get worse.

Some of us suspect that our children are drinking or using other drugs, but we do not know how to get beyond their denials, let alone how to get them to stop. We may tell ourselves that such chemical use is typical of adolescence and hope that this disturbing phase will soon pass.

Some of us acknowledge that our children have serious chemical problems that need treatment, but we do not know what kind of treatment is best, or where to find it. And even if we do, we wonder how to secure our children's cooperation.

So we reason with our children. We plead, we try to get our children to see the light. When that doesn't work, we overlook the behavior and cry ourselves to sleep at night. We nag, threaten, bribe, punish, and reward our children. We worry endlessly. We lock our children in one night, out the next. We rant and rave and tear out our hair. We try anything and everything, but nothing works.

We are not crazy, stupid, or incompetent. Most of us are caring, competent parents trying to do the best for our children in the face of seemingly insurmountable problems.

When addressing a child's use of alcohol and other drugs, you'll find that knowledge is indeed power. The purpose of this book is to provide you—the parents of children under the age of twenty-five—with that knowledge. This book will help you prevent your child from developing alcohol and other drug problems, recognize an existing chemical problem, intervene at any stage, get treatment, support your child in recovery, *and* take care of yourself.

Adolescent alcohol and drug problems are baffling, and deadly. But the proper knowledge can help you find solutions. Prevention, recognition, intervention, treatment, and recovery are possible.

No, I am not a Pollyanna. I am a psychiatric nurse and chemical dependency counselor who has worked with emotionally disturbed adolescents in a psychiatric hospital and with the chemically dependent at an in-patient treatment center. I have helped design and implement alcohol and other drug programs for junior and senior high school students. I have founded an out-patient chemical dependency center that treats persons of all ages, as well as their families, and am currently treating clients in private practice. I have also written two other books on addiction, *The Booze Battle* and *Beyond the Booze Battle*. And of one thing I am certain: *if you know what to do, you will do it*. I see that happen every day of the week, year in and year out.

In addition to being a chemical dependency expert, I am the mother of three children, now young adults. None of them has a chemical problem, but as a young adult, I did. Fortunately, I responded to treatment. So do most of the chemically dependent persons, young and old, with whom I work. From my experience, both personal and professional, I know that when chemical dependency is properly treated, recovery can be achieved.

One problem is that parents are often caught unawares. The first inkling may come when your fourteen-year-old leaves home to live with her new boyfriend, a twenty-two-year-old drug addict. Or when you walk by your son's room and see him guzzling vodka from a bottle. Or when your child is arrested for selling cocaine. Or when he threatens to stab you with a knife. Or when she fails ninth grade. Or attempts suicide.

Rarely do parents know exactly what to do. It's tempting to excuse anything suspicious as normal adolescent behavior. Feeling alone and unsure, you may do nothing. As problems continue to mount, you may begin to walk on eggs in your own home, afraid of your child's heightened hostility. Eventually parental authority may be totally relinquished as you become convinced your child cannot be helped unless he or she wants help.

This book will show you how to reclaim your parental power so you can help both your child and yourself. The first three chapters introduce various forces that affect an adolescent's development, including the positive and negative pressures imposed by peers, the normal rebellion that occurs as adolescents break away from parental control, and various pressures exerted by society. Shown as well are the lives of four kids—Toni, Brian, Ricky, and Allison—who used chemicals.

Chapters 4 through 8 describe such chemicals as cocaine, crack, Ecstasy, marijuana, and "acid," and how they are used. This section shows you how to penetrate the denial you might have about your adolescent's chemical use and how to figure out the degree of their chemical involvement. The checklists of behavior and personality changes associated with chemical dependency and signs of chemical use are provided to help you evaluate both the existence and extent of your child's involvement.

As you follow the predictable personality deteriorations in five addicted children—Brad, Mark, Kimberly, David, and JoAnn—you will meet parents who took effective action early, as well as those who, for various reasons, took action only after their child had progressed into late-stage addiction, or who delayed taking any action at all.

Chapters 9 through 12 describe available forms of chemical dependency treatment and can help you determine your child's treatment needs, as well as your own. Once you have determined the appropriate type of treatment, you will find out where to get help and how you can get even an unwilling child to enter treatment.

We follow the case histories of these addicted children as their illnesses are evaluated, needs determined, and agreements made, in one way or another, to enter various types of treatment. In Chapter 12 we meet Tim and his parents, who illustrate the problems associated with late-stage addiction and codependency. We also learn what an intervention is and how it can help to save the life of an addicted child.

The needs of recovering chemically dependent adolescents are described in Chapter 13. The final chapter provides a prescription for preventive parenting: the kind that can help children avoid harmful chemical involvements, which is also the kind of parenting that best supports chemically dependent adolescents in recovery. You also learn how the children you've met throughout the book responded to treatment.

All characters in this book represent actual case studies. To protect their anonymity, their names have been changed, while their essential experiences have been left intact. All of the teenagers, or their parents, have been clients of mine. All have been, or are, dear to me, and I hope you, too, will come to feel close to them.

Before proceeding, let me define the essential terms:

Addiction and *chemical dependency* are used interchangeably. Addicted or chemically dependent adolescents, no matter what their chemical of choice, can no longer accurately predict their future chemical use. In other words, control has been lost.

Such adolescents use chemicals when they intended not to, use more than they planned, or become involved with drugs they never wanted to use. Under chemical influence they may behave in ways they did not intend. Once an adolescent becomes addicted, intentions and actions no longer match. Furthermore, chemically dependent adolescents may be able to reduce, or even eliminate, their intake for periods of time, *but they cannot maintain the reduction or withdrawal.* They cannot stay "shaped up."

Once addicted, their urge to get high supersedes all, including the basic urge to survive. As experts in the addiction field have always known, chemically dependent persons are dealing with an urge far stronger than the cravings most of us experience from time to time. Four characteristics associated with the chemically dependent person's urge to get high have been established and are substantiated by measurable changes now being revealed through molecular studies of the brain. Once addicted, the person's urge to get high—to get the effect offered by the chemical—is *overwhelming*, *primary*, *automatic*, and *permanent*.

When addicted adolescents feel the urge to get high, they are usually *overwhelmed* by the feeling. Unable to resist it consistently, if at all, they must dampen it, satisfy it, make it go away. At this point, getting high is *primary* and supersedes family, friends, school, even self-preservation. Nothing else matters.

The urge to get high will come and go, come and go, come and go. It is *automatic*, driven from within. It can look as if addicted adolescents use chemicals in response to outside events, and they often do. But the urge to get high also operates without outside triggers. It has a life of its own and may bear no relationship to events or situations in the adolescent's life.

The urge to get high is *permanent*, indelibly etched on the addict's psyche. For the rest of their lives, addicted adolescents will have to address this urge in one way or another. With treatment, which involves abstinence from all mood-altering chemicals, the urge will diminish in both strength and frequency, and will, in time, become easily manageable. Without treatment and abstinence, the urge to get high will increase until every moment of every day is totally consumed by it.

The addict's urge to get high is far stronger than human willpower and is apparently determined by changes in the brain's neurochemical processes. While the cause of addiction is not known, it certainly has something to do with the addictive properties of the drug in question. Time and dosage, along with the environment and the age at which chemical use begins, all factor into the equation. Furthermore, addiction seems to have something to do with genetics. Some adolescents with a family history of addiction are genetically predisposed to chemical dependency in much the same way as some people are genetically predisposed to diabetes, high blood pressure, cardiac disease, and certain forms of cancer. Fortunately, like so many other illnesses, addiction can be treated without its cause being known. Also, as with other inherited illnesses, measures can be taken toward prevention.

Does "harmfully involved with chemicals" mean the same thing as "addicted"? Not necessarily.

When a person is addicted, the individual's relationship to chemicals is the number one priority, and control over use is lost. Harmful involvement indicates a dangerous use of chemicals, but one in which a person still has considerable choice or control over it. Relationships, such as those with family, school, and the future, still matter. Nevertheless, even if not addicted, adolescents can easily overdose; be killed in a car accident; encounter increasing social, legal, academic, and familial problems; and have their physical, intellectual, emotional, and spiritual development impaired, perhaps permanently, all because of their involvement with alcohol or other drugs. Consequently, adolescents with a harmful chemical involvement should *not* be allowed to continue their use.

Sometimes adolescents who show a harmful involvement with chemicals are in the "early stages of addiction"—which means that the involvement will become progressively worse unless treated. Although harmful involvement does not necessarily lead to addiction, it is *never* safe to wait. The odds are against outgrowing harmful chemical involvements without suffering serious consequences. Parents should not take that chance.

Chemical dependency represents the crossing of an invisible but very real line, from wanting a chemical to needing a chemical. There is no turning back. As they say in Alcoholics Anonymous, "Once a pickle, never a cucumber." While most adolescents and young adults favor certain chemicals, it matters little which chemical they consume. Virtually any mood-altering chemical will do once the line is crossed.

But addiction to one chemical leads to addiction to other chemicals. If a drug of choice is given up, another will soon take its place. Or if another drug is regularly added to the drug of choice, the user will soon be addicted to two or more primary chemicals of choice. Especially in chemically dependent teenagers, it is rare to find a pure alcohol addict, a pure marijuana addict, a pure cocaine addict, or a pure heroin addict. Most chemically dependent young persons are addicted to several drugs, often used in combination: to alcohol and marijuana; or to alcohol, marijuana, and cocaine; or to alcohol and cocaine; or to cocaine and heroin. Other drugs—such as mescaline, butyl nitrite, LSD, PCP, and Ecstasy—are often used as fillers, taken between drugs of choice, or as icings, taken on top of the drugs of choice.

Amazingly, adolescents can use some or all of these chemicals quite extensively without parents knowing about it. Teenagers are naturally covert; it goes with the age. But teenagers who develop harmful chemical involvements are especially covert. More than anything, they do not want their chemical use known—so they hide it well.

Yet as adolescents move into increasingly harmful chemical involvements, and especially addiction, they change in ways that are visible, predictable, and beyond their control. Addiction is the great equalizer, causing very different adolescents to become alike. As their dependency on chemicals increases, adolescent users become unable to conceal their behavioral changes.

Unfortunately, as adolescents change, so do parents. Maladaptive behavior in children causes a maladaptive response in parents—*if* parents do not receive the proper guidance. Parents are repeatedly forced to tolerate intolerable behavior, until, in time, the adolescent reigns supreme, doing whatever he wants, whenever he wants. The parents, in turn, suffer enormous guilt, shame, fear, and loss of self-esteem. Ultimately they lose their ability to view reality accurately; to them all the abnormal changes begin to seem normal.

With the guidance offered in this book, you can figure out what changes you need to make, and how to make them, so that you can reverse your child's maladaptive response. You can discover how to respond to your child in ways that enable a return to health on *both* your parts.

An old Chinese proverb says, "We see when we see." Read on; it's time to see. Once you see, you will be able to change.

Knowledge will empower you. You will no longer have to be baffled by your child's use of alcohol and other drugs. You will no longer have to feel crazy, stupid, or incompetent. You will no longer have to watch your child's behavior deteriorate.

Your child can get well, and so can you.

I wish you Godspeed—and clear vision.

The Nature of Adolescence

Deborah has a newspaper clipping, now quite yellowed, which describes an accident that occurred in her town. A car, out of control, veered into a sidewalk, hitting a young mother and her two children—an infant and a toddler—before crashing into a plate glass window. The mother and younger child were seriously injured; the older child, while not injured, was crying hysterically. All were taken by ambulance to the hospital, accompanied by two fourteen-year-old girls who had witnessed the accident. One of the teenagers stayed with the injured child in the emergency room, while the second remained with the other child in the waiting room. Both offered comfort for several hours while the mother was being operated on and relatives were located. One of the teenagers was Deborah's daughter, Toni.

"The whole thing just blew me away when I heard about it," Deborah recalled. "At first, I felt a need to comfort Toni. She must have been so scared herself. Mostly, though, I was proud of her . . . so in awe that she had extended herself like that. It was weird. At home it was a major ordeal to get her to set the table. All she seemed to think about was which pair of jeans to wear—and suddenly she's the town heroine. I knew all along that Toni was a caring person, but I had no idea she was that mature.''

Deborah also had no idea that it was just a matter of weeks before Toni would run away from home.

Teenagers are roses unfolding, but sometimes it's hard to see beyond the thorns. Because adolescents, especially those about twelve to fourteen, are usually rebellious.

Younger children are content to inhabit the same social world as their parents, where their range of activities is fairly restricted. They do not have the will, strength, or social capacity to challenge these restrictions. Lacking the techniques for independent survival, they have an overpowering need for close contact with powerful, sheltering, nurturing parents. Consequently, young children are geared toward maintaining the status quo along with their parents.

But as young children approach the age of eleven, they begin to chafe at the bit. Moving from being conforming, dependent children to being independent, initiating, and coping adults, they become increasingly uncomfortable with the restrictions of family life. And so adolescence involves changing the status quo.

This process involves two basic maturative tasks. First, adolescents must find their own identity and come to know and feel comfortable with the uniqueness, separateness, and wholeness of their own selves. Second, they must free themselves from attachments to their parents by developing the coping skills necessary for independence, which includes being responsible for their own behavior. Thus can adolescents gradually assume the autonomy necessary for healthy adult life.

The adolescent's journey toward autonomy begins with small steps, which, to him, are endeavors of the highest order. "Why do I always have to take the garbage out?" "I don't want to go to church." "Why should I make my bed?

It's just going to get messed up again!'' "But I have to make one more call.'' "I think better with the TV on.'' "School sucks.'' "This whole family sucks.'' "It's not my turn to do the dishes.'' "Why can't I? Everyone else can.'' On and on it goes. The bickering can seem endless; it's incredibly irritating to parents. But, important as it is, that is all it really is— bickering, chronic infighting over day-to-day issues. Tugs at the apron strings. Thorns of adolescence.

Such tugs indicate that the young person is going through a negative dependency stage—a to-be-expected normal stage in which the adolescent's decisions and actions are based on the negative of his parents' wishes, rather than on his own positive desires. If his parents want him to turn the music down so he can study, he says he can't concentrate unless it's blaring. If they want him to get some new clothes, he's happy with the ones he has. That old saw about getting a thirteen-year-old to do something by pretending you want the opposite isn't far off the mark. The young adolescent's continuing dependency is readily apparent, as is his emerging emancipation: what he thinks and does is based on his parents' opinions and suggestions, but in the reverse.

This can produce considerable turmoil within the family; young adolescents are seldom gracious in their attempts at rebellion. Since parents are used to being minded, needed, even adored, they also are not necessarily at their best in the face of their children's rebellion. As a result, each generation can easily inflame the other. While each is fearful of the resulting outbreaks, most of the time both the individuals and the family as a whole come out of the turmoil intact, even strengthened. While the reasons for why adolescents and parents fight are often insignificant, the rebellion itself is of monumental importance. It is the initial stage of the adolescent's emancipation.

■ ■

Toni, the town heroine, went to great lengths to secure her independence from her mother, although her rebellion started gradually. Each morning, when eleven-year-old Toni skipped down the hill and across the neighbors' lawns to school, she would slow down only as she reached the bleachers alongside the football field, where the older boys stood under the bleachers, smoking marijuana. When she ran by, they would call out, teasing and scaring her. They seemed to do that mostly when she ran, so often she would walk. She hated these high school boys for scaring her and decided smoking pot was bad.

Two years later, when she was thirteen and beginning eighth grade, so many kids in her school were drinking beer and smoking pot that Toni began to see it as normal. "I really began to wonder how something could be so bad if that many kids were doing it."

So during a snowstorm later that winter, Toni shared a couple of six-packs of beer with two of her friends. "But then I got scared because I didn't know what was happening to me. I decided I should go home—though that really didn't make any sense, because I knew my mother was home and would freak if she found out I'd been drinking. I headed home anyway, right out into the blizzard. On the way, I slipped on some ice and hurt my ankle. It was dark and windy and snowing so hard I could barely see. I started to cry. My ankle was killing me and I guess I thought I was going to die out there on that road. I started crawling, pulling myself along, and finally made it to a neighbor's house. He called my mom and they took me to the emergency room. When it turned out I had broken my leg, my mom cried because she felt sorry for me. But when she hugged me and got a whiff of my breath, she freaked. She hissed at me and accused me of drinking. I lied and said I hadn't been drinking, but she said the whole world could smell it. I still lied and she hissed even louder.

"The whole scene was a nightmare. I'm flat out on the examining table, my leg's throbbing, and I'm still drunk. The walls are going around in circles, and I'm beginning to feel sick to my stomach. My mom's standing there, staring down at me like I'm the scum of the earth, and I'm wishing I was back out in the blizzard.

"Later, when my mom was helping me into bed, she hugged me and started crying. She said she was sorry, that she shouldn't have spoken to me like that. She told me she loved me and wasn't angry anymore. I told her I had been drinking and that I was sorry for lying to her. We talked a long time. She told me we have relatives who are alcoholics, which puts us at high risk. She said it didn't mean I couldn't drink, but that I'd be safer if I put off drinking until I was older, and asked me not to drink until I was of legal drinking age. I agreed.

"My mom said something else that night that I've never forgotten. I told her that maybe the reason I broke my ankle was because God was punishing me for drinking. I'll never forget her answer. She said that God didn't make me fall; the beer made me fall; that I was drunk, and that's why I was out in the blizzard in the first place. It was true. I was in a cast and on crutches for three months and all that time, every day, I had a vivid reminder about how strong alcohol can be.

"I never got into pot. I tried it in eighth grade, but it always made me feel weird, out of control. My life was getting messed up around that time, and I didn't need something like pot to mess it up even more.

"I've never had a good relationship with my father, and everything seemed to get worse when I became a teenager. My parents got divorced when I was seven, and even though I saw my dad a lot, I was always tense when I was with him. I never knew what kind of mood he'd be in and I always felt like I had to do things to please him, or he'd be angry. Now

I really don't expect much from him, but when I was younger, I expected a lot and got hurt a lot. Every time I knew I was going to see him, I'd think, 'This time it'll be different,' but it never was.

"It was after I started therapy that I learned my father's moods were his problem, not mine . . . that I wasn't causing them, that his moods didn't mean there was something wrong with me. I think I already knew that, though, because my mom was so caring. She wasn't moody and she made me feel like she valued me as a person. But in junior high school I started fighting with her a lot, and that's when I started feeling messed up.

"You see, when my mom put her foot down, it stayed down. My brother and sister didn't seem to mind it so much, but I was as stubborn as she was. It made us fight a lot. It was really rough for a year or so . . . a lot of times I hated her. Then one night she pushed too far.

"It was a few months after I'd gotten off the crutches and I'd stayed out beyond my curfew. We'd been fighting more than usual about one thing or another, and that night was just too much. We were both screaming at each other and she told me if I wasn't willing to follow the rules of our home, I could find another home. I went up to my room and waited till I thought she was asleep. Then I called a friend of mine and talked her into running away with me. I snuck out of the house, met my friend, and we went down to the taxi stand where we hired a limo to drive us into Greenwich Village in New York City. We charged the limo to my mom's account, and that made me feel real good. When we got to the Village, we just walked around playing like we were having fun, but the truth is, we were both scared. By then it was about three or four in the morning. We had just enough money to get to Grand Central and take the first train out that morning back to our town.

"I was too scared to go home, so we went to my friend's house. Her mom cried and hugged us and told us how glad she was we were safe. So then I called my mom. I was feeling guilty, you know, sorry I had caused her so much worry. What a blow! When I told my mom I was safe at Jan's and that I'd be right home, she said she was happy I was safe but that she wasn't ready to have me come home. She asked me to meet her later that day at Joe's, a local coffee shop. I hung up on her! I was so furious that I never wanted to see her again, but she called right back and said she was taking the day off from work to do something important which concerned both of us and asked if I'd meet her later that afternoon to talk about it. So I did. She didn't give me much choice, and besides, I wanted to find out what she was up to.

"At Joe's we didn't hug each other like we usually did. I guess we were both still angry, still hurting. My mom said she needed help. She knew things were wrong between us, and she wanted help so she could find out how to make things better. She'd just seen a therapist and asked if I'd be willing to get help with her. Would I! I was thrilled! I was so grateful she was shouldering some of the responsibility, that she was admitting she wasn't perfect. I knew I was causing a lot of problems, but I also knew it wasn't only me at fault. When I saw she was willing to look at herself, I would have done anything for her. We hugged and cried and hugged some more, right there in the coffee shop.

"Even with therapy my mom was still strict, but she started negotiating with us a lot more. We got into being more responsible because that's what we really wanted, and my mom became more trusting. The tension in our family went away, and it was great feeling loved and having fun again. I'm really glad my mom got the help for all of us when she did, because I think we were at a crucial point in our lives. Things could have gotten so much worse instead of better."

■ ■

Usually the process of emancipation, the unhooking from parents, is more gradual. Crises tend to be more transitory, seldom of the all-or-none nature as experienced by Toni and her mother, Deborah. Their "follow-the-rules-or-find-another-home" crisis led them to a total break; luckily, each quickly took action to repair the rupture and to ensure that it did not occur again in the future.

Deborah said that, during the years her children were adolescents, she often felt as if she was walking a fine line. "It was a scary period. Hardly a week went by without hearing about another kid overdosing, or committing suicide, or smashing up a car while drunk. And the town we lived in was crazy, just crazy, the way it handled the adolescent drug problem.

"Every spring the eighth graders had a formal dinner dance, and every year the parents would titter when some of the kids got drunk. They thought it was cute. Even after our state raised the legal drinking age to twenty-one, the school continued to give beer steins to the graduating eighteen-year-old seniors. And once, when the coaches kicked some of the kids off the football team for drinking, a whole group of parents got in an uproar. I swear to God, they actually insisted the 'no-chemical-use' pledges taken by the athletes were made to be broken! The school buckled and the players were reinstated.

"The point is, I knew I was bucking a system that condoned what I considered aberrant adolescent behavior. The other parents talked against drugs, but few seemed to take alcohol seriously.

"That's another reason that I knew I needed help after Toni took off that night. I was sure I'd never be able to buck the system in our town unless I was functioning very well with my own kids. And obviously I wasn't, if I'd reached the point of screaming at my own budding adolescent daughter to find another home.

"That night was a terror. I was petrified. I called the local police as soon as I realized Toni had taken off. They tracked her to the limo stand, so I knew she was in the heart of New York City—not exactly where you want your fourteen-year-old daughter to be in the middle of the night. The New York police wouldn't put out a missing person alert for several hours, so there was nothing I could do. Jan's parents were also at their wits' end.

"I felt like I was between a rock and a hard place. I wanted Toni home more than anything in the world, but I also knew there was no way we could live together if she wasn't willing to follow the rules of the household. All that night, in between praying for her safety, I kept asking myself that if I'd reached this impossible point at the *beginning* of my children's adolescence, what in the world would I be doing as they got older?

"It was very clear to me that I needed help. After all, I was the one who had taken us to the all-or-none position. But, since I knew this crisis really affected all of us, I concentrated on therapy for our whole family. I knew, without any doubt, that how we managed this crisis could make us or break us. So when Toni finally called, I knew exactly what to do."

As the story of Toni and Deborah demonstrates, the resolution is often more important than the conflict. One way or another, most adolescents and their parents, like Toni and Deborah, effect resolutions that pave the way to a gradual, ever-so-slow, unhooking from parental controls.

Usually, too, adolescents accomplish their emancipation without having to reject their parents completely. In fact, while fighting over inconsequential issues, adolescents retain much of their parents' value system. Although adults become a general irritant to them, adolescents will respect parental opinions at the same time. They rail against, but do not totally reject.

Just as their behavior starts to change, so do their bodies. Young adolescents are zapped with new hormones that cause great physical changes. They experience surges of growth, especially in their extremities—neck, arms, legs—making them feel and look coltish, awkward, or gawky. Sex organs also develop, particularly genitalia in boys and breasts in girls. They sweat differently, and body odor develops. Blackheads and pimples pop up. New sexual juices flow. Voices squeak in boys and menses start in girls. The changes seem to occur so rapidly that they hardly know what to expect upon awakening each morning.

Not surprisingly, young adolescents become enormously preoccupied with their bodies to the exclusion of almost everything else. Attempting to distract a thirteen-year-old Toni one evening, Deborah spoke about her fears of the U.S. involvement in Nicaragua and asked her daughter for her views. Toni's only response was, "Mom, tell me the truth, the absolute truth. Does my hair look better like this or the way I wore it yesterday?" So much for Nicaragua. Parents can easily lose their patience with such self-involvement, calling their children vain one moment, while bemoaning their appearance the next.

Since being okay to young adolescents means being the same as every other twelve-year-old, any deviation from the norm may very well add a sense of shame to a child's existing sense of awkwardness. Under any conditions, young adolescents are incredibly sensitive. Now, with these bodily changes, there is hardly anything their parents can do or say to please them.

Bothersome as it may be, neither the preoccupation with their own bodies nor the negative dependent behavior they exhibit in early adolescence lasts long. By the time adolescents enter high school, the infighting over day-to-day issues becomes less acute and the self-centeredness less total. Then a more peaceful period, a moratorium of sorts, is entered as adolescents move on to new concerns and horizons, expand their abilities, activities, and interests, and try to find themselves in the world. Rather than having any specific developmental stages through which they must navigate, fifteen-, sixteen-, and seventeen-year-olds focus on consolidating their identities and achieving autonomy and independence.

Parents should bear in mind that healthy adolescents *of any age* do not consistently manifest deviant behavior by breaking rules at home, in school, or in the world at large. Unhealthy adolescents, particularly adolescents who have developed a harmful involvement with chemicals, *do* manifest such behavior, and are in need of both diagnostic evaluation and treatment.

I must admit that my work with disturbed adolescents initially led me to believe that all teenagers are mixed up in one way or another. Hearing parents just about everywhere say ''he'll outgrow it'' persuaded me that disturbed behavior is to be expected. But my own three children, as well as the secondary school students and chemically dependent adolescents in recovery with whom I have worked, have taught me otherwise.

Most teenagers are *not* mixed up. When adolescents appear disturbed, they *are* disturbed. They may outgrow it—but then again, they may not. It took being with healthy teenagers for me to accept fully what both teachers and social scientists have been saying all along: adolescence is marked by emotional health, not illness.

Let me reiterate that *adolescents normally do not demonstrate any repeated or seriously deviant behavior at home or at school*. Like Toni, most adolescents may have one or two major rebellious outbreaks, but overall they present a pattern of consistency, remaining true to their basic natures as they progress through childhood to adolescence and finally adulthood. *They do not become* different people—strangers to their parents, or delinquents—simply because they become teenagers. Adolescence should be a period of growth undergone without serious disruptions between the generations, or between the adolescent and his former identity.

Generally speaking, teenagers are remarkably flexible and stable. It is true that they need to be active, and that they experience sharp, intense emotions, often marked by exuberance and elation or anxiety and anguish. Yet they are quick to recognize their feelings and can cope effectively with only a moderate amount of brooding or reflection.

Healthy teenagers present their parents with wonderful gifts. Leaving behind the self-centeredness and concrete thinking of their early childhood, they show compassion for others and develop expanded interests, including working toward their futures. Outgrowing the dependencies of their youth, they begin to assume responsibility for their own behavior and develop new coping skills, which are often astonishing. They become caring, giving, responsible, and competent.

T W O

Peer Groups

A key to understanding the adolescent's self-perception is to recognize his pervasive feeling of being out of step—with his peers, the adult world, even his own body. With one foot in the adult world and one still in the world of the child, the adolescent's status is ambiguous; he is neither here nor there. To get "in step," most teenagers devote considerable energies to gaining peer acceptance. Since they are not yet comfortable with themselves, they have a strong need to be accepted by their peers. And to be accepted, they feel they have to be just like their peers.

Brian felt that he was different and had many problems gaining his peers' acceptance. When he recalls his junior high school years, in which he characterizes himself as "too dumb, too short, and way behind everyone," his smile fades and his words falter. "It was like I was invisible. No one noticed me, or if they did, they put me down. The cafeteria was the worst. Either I sat on the fringe of a group, not really belonging, or I sat alone. Either way, I felt out of it, and I always had the idea that every kid in the cafeteria was watching me be all alone."

Wanting to be liked, Brian had his first taste of alcohol in eighth grade. "Two of my buddies and I stood outside the supermarket one night and when an older woman, twenty-five or so, came along, we gave her money and asked her to buy us each a six-pack. I got drunk. At the time, it seemed like a lot of fun, and I stayed at my friend's house so my parents wouldn't find out I'd been drinking.

"The truth is, those guys weren't really my friends. I didn't have any. The only reason they were with me is because I promised I'd pay for the beer. I bought friends a lot in those days . . . mostly by supplying the money for booze."

Brian says his parents were very clear about their expectations regarding alcohol and drug use. "Neither was allowed. My parents don't use drugs of any kind, and they don't drink all that much either. Sometimes my mom has a glass of wine when they go out to dinner, and my dad has a beer. But they're just not into alcohol, and they made it very clear that they didn't want me into it either. But you almost couldn't *not* drink in my town. From eighth grade on, there were parties every weekend; at every party there was alcohol." Despite his parents' wishes, Brian started drinking beer on the weekends in high school. "It was the thing to do. Besides, if I wanted friends, it was the only thing to do."

Brian also started smoking marijuana about the same time, "so the other kids would like me. Besides, pot was all over the place, and, you know, you want to try it to see what it feels like. I loved it. By my sophomore year, I was smoking two or three times a week. But I always felt guilty afterwards. I was always afraid my parents would find out. Like I said, my parents are really solid. I mean, they don't go around popping Valium like some parents I know. They're into functioning . . . you know, living a decent life."

Brian reports that he never tried other drugs. "There was a lot of other stuff around—acid, Quaaludes, coke—but that's where I drew the line. I was already feeling guilty about doing dope [marijuana]. No way was I going further than that. Then I stopped smoking pot the end of my sophomore year.

"Why? Well . . . uh . . . all hell broke loose, that's why. My mom found my stash [supply of marijuana] in a pair of jeans when she was doing the laundry and told my dad. Jesus, you should have seen him. I was at school that evening, practicing for the spring play, and Dad marched in. I mean, he charged down that aisle like a bull, right up to the foot of the stage. We all stopped to watch, and he looked up at me like he could've killed me. He told me to get my stuff and come home with him. I was embarrassed as hell, but mostly I was afraid to get in the car with him. I knew he'd caught me at something, and I was pretty sure it was the pot. I had to take his angry silence all the way home. I mean, I was scared! You don't know what his silence is like. My dad's never been physically violent; he never even shouts. But I can tell you, when you get his silent treatment, you're out there all alone in the cold . . . totally abandoned. That's when shouting looks pretty good. At least then you'd feel connected.

"I wanted to crawl into a hole that night, to get away from him . . . his silence, but I couldn't. When we finally got home, he told me to be up, showered, dressed, and ready for school by 5:30 the next morning so he could talk to me before he left for work. That's one morning I didn't oversleep, that's for sure.

"We sat down, over the Cheerios, just the two of us. Jesus! I wanted to run. He told me some stuff about loving me and caring about my future. He said he had no intention of watching me blow it away with alcohol or drugs. He made it very clear that both were absolutely forbidden, and that if I drank or smoked pot again, I'd face severe consequences, like having the things I really liked taken away. Then he grounded me for a couple of weeks and asked which I wanted to give up over the next two weeks, hockey or music. At first, I couldn't believe that my dad would actually go to the school and ask the coach to suspend me from the team because I'd used pot, but when I thought about it, I knew that's exactly what he'd do. My dad doesn't horse around. So I chose to give up listening to my music. No way did I want the coach or the team involved.

"After that, when I was no longer drinking or doing dope, I really had to work at being accepted. Being good at a sport helped, but I felt pretty lonely for a while."

These days, Brian seems pretty secure. Although he's not too sure what he's going to do when he finishes college in a few months, he's not too worried. He knows he'll luck onto something.

While Brian believes he has been lucky in life, others in his position might disagree. Brian has two older brothers, each over six feet tall; Brian is five feet five inches, "when I stretch a bit." One of his brothers has a doctorate in applied mathematics; the other is studying biophysics at Massachusetts Institute of Technology. Both are intellectually gifted; Brian has an average IQ and has suffered from learning disabilities as far back as he can remember. He says, "It's the D's that bother me, not the C's."

In fact, too many D's got Brian suspended from college during his second year. "But I talked to the dean. I really believed I had a good case. I didn't take basket weaving, the easy courses. I told him a D in physics meant more to me than an A in pottery. He gave me another chance. I've gone through college on probation practically every semester, but you know what? I'm getting a good education."

When asked how he feels about his smaller stature, he said, "Better me than them. My brothers are bright, but they're thin-skinned. They wouldn't have been able to take being short. Anyhow, what does it matter? So I don't play basketball, but I've played varsity hockey for the past six years. I love music. I don't need to be tall to attend concerts and play my guitar. I have lots of friends, and they don't seem to care if I'm short.

"Besides, I've got a great girl. So you see, I'm really lucky.

She's terrific. If she isn't the most beautiful girl in my school, she's close to it. She's everything I've ever wanted, and she loves me. She still gets drunk a little too often, but she's only a sophomore. I figure she's got a few more times to get drunk in her. It takes until about your junior year to see that getting drunk, getting sick, and vomiting all over everyone isn't all that much fun. I can't even remember the last time I got bombed.''

Not all teenagers exert pressure on their peers to drink or do drugs, as in Brian's case. Instead, many encourage their friends to steer away from heavy chemical use.

Toni reports that several of her friends occasionally drank beer at parties, but not enough to get drunk. "Except for my friend Cathy. At about every party, she just wouldn't stop at one or two beers. I mean, she was a mess—vomiting all over, passing out. So finally we put it to her: either she limited her drinking, or we weren't going to take her to parties with us. She shaped up. I guess she didn't want to lose us and I'm glad, because I really liked Cathy a lot.''

As children enter high school, there is often a shifting about of friendships—a moving about among peers as they search for groups in which they feel most at home. If adolescents are not yet into regular chemical use, as a rule they will not be especially welcomed by, nor feel comfortable with, their chemical-using peers. Generally they will seek out peers who abstain, or who drink moderately as they do. Yet sometimes, in order to be accepted, they will conform, even if this leads to grossly deviant behavior.

Ricky's group of friends from junior high remained pretty much intact when they entered high school. That's where he said he felt good about himself—with his old buddies—and he stayed a part of the group, even when they began to experiment with heroin.

Ricky is not here to tell his story. He died last year of an apparently inadvertent overdose, despite his parents' efforts (many of which were, unfortunately, misguided).

When Ramona and Jim, Ricky's parents, first came to me for help, Ricky was an eighteen-year-old high school dropout who had been a heroin addict for at least three years. He was not working and was living at home. He frequently stole from his parents—televisions, radios, jewelry, stereo, clothes, anything remotely "hockable." He often begged his parents for money; if they were not immediately forthcoming, he verbally abused them, kicked holes in the walls, or broke furniture. Once, in the throes of heroin withdrawal, Ricky looked so pathetic and desperate—having dry heaves and severe abdominal cramps—that Jim actually went to buy heroin at an address Ricky supplied. Back at home, Jim followed Ricky's instructions, prepared the heroin, and helped Ricky with the injection. "That's when I knew we needed help," Jim admitted.

"I knew we needed help long before that, but no one listened," Ramona added.

While Ramona and Jim often seemed at odds with each other, both agreed that Ricky, the older of their two children, had always been a quiet child. "The only thing we ever worried about was that he seemed to be a follower. He just tagged along," Jim recalled.

Ramona had found a syringe on Ricky's dresser when he was fifteen. Ricky had protested then that he had no idea where it had come from. Ramona and Jim were suspicious. "A couple of his friends had been busted for heroin possession, and sometimes Ricky looked drugged. But we couldn't get him to stop hanging around with those guys. He kept promising us he'd never use heroin, but obviously he didn't keep his promises," Jim explained.

"He was always so shy," Ramona went on, "that I felt sorry for him. Then when he stopped going to school—he just refused to go anymore—I thought he needed friends more than ever, but I knew he didn't have much of a chance of finding new ones. So sometimes, when I knew he was with his old friends, I wouldn't tell Jim. Besides, I was afraid; sometimes Jim beat up on Ricky.''

"Yeah? And what'd you do?'' Jim angrily retorted. "You let him get away with everything.''

Jim is a self-made man. His father died of alcoholism when Jim was eleven, and he had to help support his mother and three younger siblings. After finishing high school, he joined the New York City Fire Department, and is still a fire fighter. While by no means wealthy, Jim is proud of being able to offer his family the comforts that he never received as a child.

Because he had overcome so many obstacles, Jim couldn't see why Ricky couldn't do the same. Even when he finally knew Ricky was using heroin, it didn't occur to him to offer Ricky treatment. Instead he cajoled, threatened, and bullied, exhorting Ricky to use willpower. Frustrated by Ricky's inability to help himself, Jim sometimes hit Ricky, or went to the opposite extremes of either overlooking Ricky's behavior or actually securing heroin for him.

Ramona prided herself on having been a good mother when her children were little. What she didn't realize was that she was *too* good. Even when they grew old enough to do for themselves, she never asked her sons to help with household chores or to assume responsibilities of any kind. If they missed curfews, she readily accepted their explanations. If they didn't do their homework, she did it for them. When Ricky started cutting classes, and then whole days, she wrote excuses for him. Her children were her world; more than anything, she wanted them to be happy.

Needless to say, Jim's brand of parenting caused Ramona great discomfort. Their two styles clashed; he became more bullying and she continued to pamper. But by now they were scared enough to work together. They gathered a team of family members, did an intervention (explained further in Chapter 12), and got Ricky to agree to enter a long-term residential treatment center in another part of the state, far away from his addicted friends. Ricky stayed at the center for only three weeks. Even though he had not completed treatment, Ramona and Jim welcomed him back, with the understanding that he would not use heroin. Shortly thereafter, when the pupils of Ricky's eyes were constricted to pinpoints and he was nodding out in the middle of conversations, Ramona and Jim once again offered help.

When he refused, they took one of the bravest actions of their lives. They kicked Ricky out of their apartment, changed their locks, and called the police each time Ricky tried to break in. They continued to tell Ricky that they were willing to help him, but only if he agreed to return to treatment.

After about a month, Ramona and Jim dropped out of my parent therapy group. Not long afterwards, other parents in the group who'd kept in touch with Ramona and Jim reported that they had allowed Ricky back into their home, even though he was still using heroin and refusing treatment. It wasn't much later that Ramona found Ricky sprawled dead on the bathroom floor, a syringe dangling from a vein in his groin.

It is true, of course, that Ramona and Jim took a long time seeking help in order to confront Ricky's addiction effectively and that they did not follow through. But it is also true that Ricky was by nature a passive child, a follower, and such adolescents are powerfully influenced by their peers.

Yes, peer groups are risky. But they are a vital and indisputable part of adolescent life. Adolescents can find answers to "Who am I?," "What kind of person am I?," "What can kids my age do?," and "What am I capable of?" through peer group membership. A peer group offers adolescents ready support. It reassures them that they are okay. It helps them feel understood. It helps them understand themselves. A peer group offers adolescents a sense of belonging, the knowledge that they are not all alone. A peer group offers guidance. It provides points of identification. It helps validate adolescents' perceptions of reality.

Within a peer group, adolescents can try out new roles—budding physicist or all-time jock, punk or preppy. They can test new names, exotic looks, and different hairstyles. They can, and do, evaluate these new roles and styles in front of their own mirror, but they also seek reactions from others, with the most valued reactions coming from their peers. After all, what do parents know? They're only parents.

Within peer groups, adolescents can try out roles without any permanent commitment. Both peers and parents perceive this experimentation as a severing of childhood dependencies rather than as a prelude to anything lasting—but peers are likely to take it seriously, while parents often take it lightly.

Peer groups can ease adolescents' anxieties about becoming responsible members of the adult world. Nevertheless, peer groups are often a major source of conflict and stress for teenagers. While trying to find an identity outside their family, adolescents risk not being welcomed in the group. And while trying to become free of family ties, adolescents risk becoming captive to another set of behavior-controlling standards. Adolescents must struggle with the peer group's inherent tyranny—"You need us"—as well as its power to intimidate through ridicule and rejection if its rules are not followed. And rule number one is "Do not be different."

Brian broke the rule by being different, and he broke it again when he gave up alcohol and marijuana after being confronted by his father. No longer a user, he was dropped by the friends he had found through using. When asked where he got the strength to persevere until he found new friends, Brian seemed to draw a blank. He said he knew it took strength, which he feels he was probably born with, but he expressed surprise at hearing he had options other than perseverance. While he was willing to give up alcohol and marijuana to regain parental approval, he was not willing to forgo peer approval simply because he was no longer using chemicals. For example, it never occurred to Brian to give up and become a loner or to get involved in an ever-increasing number of self-destructive actions in order to impress others. Yet, in the face of the peer rejection and ridicule Brian experienced, others without his personal resources might well have succumbed to such options.

Individuals without such strength and perseverance will need considerable parental support to guide them safely through their adolescence. Guidelines for creating such support are described in Chapter 14.

Keep in mind that peer groups can be either a constructive force, which helps your child progress toward adulthood, or a destructive influence. Healthy peer groups enable teenagers to enlarge their identity by developing a keen sense of social self outside family limits. They provide a context for participation in all kinds of constructive school and community activities. Members of healthy peer groups do function within the rules and norms of society.

Unfortunately, unhealthy peer groups perpetuate unresolved emotional dependencies left over from childhood, which are then often manifested in massive anticonformity and in the abuse of alcohol and other drugs. Unhealthy peer groups promote aberrant, deviant behavior; their members, often characterized as "losers," are frequently in trouble in school, in the community, and with the law. Rather than being a vital part of the maturation process, such groups short-circuit an adolescent's emancipation. Let's make sure this does not happen to *your* child.

THREE

The Choices Kids Must Make in Today's World

Allison was in fifth grade when she had her first beer. Two years later, she began to show the behavior/personality changes associated with an adolescent's harmful chemical involvement.

According to her parents, Phyllis and Stuart, Allison had always been a model child—an excellent student, popular with her teachers and other children, cheerful, polite, and interested in sports and animals. But last year all that began to change. "Now it's like she's a totally different child," Phyllis said.

Phyllis and Stuart were high school sweethearts who married after college and returned to their hometown, where Phyllis taught school and Stuart worked in his family's lumber business. Allison was born three years later, and Melissa followed two years after that.

Phyllis had stayed home "to be a full-time mother" during the girls' preschool years. She reported, "Both babies were perfect—happy, healthy, bouncy, beautiful—everything we'd ever wanted. Those years were great. In fact, everything was great right up until two years ago. We used to have fun. We did a lot together as a family, right, Stu? Remember the laughs, the love we shared? Now all that's changed. Stu sits off in the den hidden behind his computer. Melissa slinks off by herself. I cry and nag and then nag some more. And God knows what Allison's up to. Most of the time she's holed up in her room . . . when she's home, that is.''

Within weeks of starting seventh grade, Allison was bringing home C's and D's instead of A's and B's. The school complained because Allison was frequently tardy, was not completing her homework, and was talking back to teachers. At one interview, Phyllis and Stuart were told that Allison was hanging around with the ''wrong'' crowd, a group of eighth graders known to be ''troubled'' students.

At home Allison had become surly and sullen. ''She would literally snarl at us. She started swearing a lot and would fly off into screaming rages, the likes of which I'd never seen,'' Phyllis lamented. ''The least little thing would tick her off. And she began to spend a lot of time in her room. She wouldn't even bother talking to us at meals. She became a stranger; I felt like I didn't know her anymore.''

Once, when Phyllis picked Allison up from a friend's house, she thought she smelled alcohol on Allison's breath. Later that evening, she and Stuart checked their liquor supply—which they rarely touched—and found several nearly empty bottles. The next day Phyllis searched Allison's room. She found an empty bottle of vodka at the bottom of the clothes hamper in her closet.

''I was so scared, I was shaking,'' Phyllis admitted. ''One night, a couple of weeks earlier, Allison had come home drunk from a party. She was so stupefied she could barely stand up. Stu and I were upset then, but not this upset. Thinking of her drinking beer with friends at a party was one thing; thinking of her drinking hard liquor all by herself was another matter altogether.

''I took the rest of the day off and went over to the lumberyard to tell Stu. Neither of us could believe it. We were worried to death. One of Stu's uncles had died from alcoholism and so had my grandfather. We know, of course, that alcoholism can be passed on genetically, but somehow we never thought it would happen to our kids—I guess because it hadn't happened to us. Still, at that point, we weren't really thinking about alcoholism. We were more concerned about finding out from Allison what was going on and getting her to stop drinking.''

Allison was indignant that evening when Phyllis and Stuart confronted her. Denying everything, she said she hadn't been drinking, that Phyllis couldn't possibly have smelled alcohol on her breath, that she didn't even know they had alcohol in the house. As for the vodka bottle in her hamper, ''Someone else must have put it there.'' Then she started screaming at her parents for searching her room and invading her privacy. She accused them of being ''stinking, rotten'' parents who didn't know how to be parents because they didn't even know how to trust. She ended her tirade with a threat: ''If you're not going to trust me, I'll go someplace else where they will trust me.'' And she stomped out of the room.

Phyllis and Stuart were shocked. Phyllis cried and Stuart consoled her. Neither knew what to do next but finally decided that in the morning they'd try to get Allison to promise not to drink. Phyllis also wanted to ground Allison for her verbally abusive behavior. Believing this would only anger Allison further, Stuart felt they should concentrate solely on the drinking problem. But Phyllis insisted that both the drinking and the verbal abuse were problems and should be addressed.

When confronted, Allison was, at first, contrite. She apologized for her behavior of the night before and promised not to drink anymore. Then she asked that her mother promise not to search her room. Phyllis agreed to this—unless she saw reason to search it, such as alcohol on Allison's breath. Allison countered angrily, saying she promised not to drink—unless she saw reason to drink, like a snooping mother. Screaming at Phyllis and calling her a "fucking bitch," Allison told her mother that she hated her, grabbed her coat, and marched out of the house. Phyllis yelled at her to get back in the house, but Allison marched on.

Phyllis put her head down on the table and wept. Stuart tried to soothe her, but he also told her that she'd made matters worse. He thought that since Allison had promised not to drink, Phyllis should have promised not to search her room. While that didn't sound quite right to Phyllis, she agreed that she had not handled things well. "It was like nothing I did was right anymore," she said. Finally they agreed to ground Allison for that morning's verbal abuse. That evening, Allison quietly accepted the punishment, as if she knew she deserved it.

Over the next several weeks, Allison's behavior was erratic. At times she acted like her former friendly self, but at other times she was sullen and aloof. Occasionally she erupted violently. Phyllis noticed that Allison chewed gum a lot, but she didn't smell alcohol on her daughter's breath nor did she come across any other evidence of drinking.

Nevertheless, since neither Allison's behavior nor her grades showed any consistent improvement, Phyllis and Stuart decided to transfer Allison to parochial school. When they told Allison, she screamed, threatened, and then pleaded, promising to do everything her parents wanted. Phyllis and Stuart told Allison that if she dropped her new "troubled" friends, picked up her grades, thoroughly completed her homework assignments, had no further violent verbal or physical outbursts, and did not drink or use drugs, they would reconsider.

Allison shaped up during the last quarter of seventh grade. She got A's and B's, joined the track team, socialized with her former friends, and reverted to the Allison her parents had always known—laughing, loving, industrious, cooperative—a pleasure in virtually every way. At the end of the school year, Phyllis and Stuart told Allison that she could stay in public school. Delighted, Allison gave them each a hug and promised to continue her present behavior.

Three weeks later, she was expelled from summer camp for drinking alcohol.

Phyllis and Stuart felt at a total loss. Neither had ever faced problems they couldn't resolve. They loved each other, their children, their own parents, and their work. Both were active in their church and community, and had a wide circle of friends. They had always felt enriched—but now they felt diminished, as if they themselves were failures.

Unable to agree on what to do, they consulted their parents, Allison's pediatrician, the school psychologist, and various friends. Some, like Phyllis, thought the parochial school's stricter environment would be best for Allison. Others supported Stuart's inclination to hold parochial school over Allison's head to get her to do well in public school. Several suggested that perhaps Allison needed more freedom and that Phyllis should loosen the reins. Others suggested more discipline or perhaps getting Allison into therapy. While all gave conflicting advice, virtually everyone agreed on one thing: that they didn't really know what would be best. Despite the fact that they did not get the answers they needed, both Phyllis and Stuart were glad they had shared their problems. They felt less alone, less like failures.

During this time Phyllis was noticing other worrisome behavior. While Allison had never been particularly neat, her room was now in shambles. Laundry was strewn about, and soiled sanitary pads were left lying amid scattered magazines, books, scraps of food, tapes, and clothes. Phyllis and Allison frequently engaged in screaming tirades about the situation.

"My mother was shocked when she saw Allison's room,"

Phyllis recalled. "I took her up on her offer to speak to Allison because I thought if Allison would listen to anyone, it would be my mom; they'd always been very close. I'm really sorry now that I put my mom in that spot, because Allison raged at her. God! It was terrible! I hated Allison at that point. How could she do that to someone who had always adored her?"

Allison was also treating Melissa, her younger sister, in a tyrannical manner. She often ordered Melissa about, viciously berated her for not doing anything right, and accused her of always being in the way. On one occasion Allison pummeled Melissa so severely that she gave her several bruises.

As a result of this abusive behavior, Allison was transferred to the parochial school. But Allison resisted seeing a therapist, maintaining she didn't need treatment. She promised to prove it by being cooperative both at home and at school. Her parents relented. Allison also extracted a promise from her parents that they would let her return to the public school the following year if all went well in eighth grade.

While not completely her old self, Allison was not as sullen and combative as in the past. She rarely erupted violently and was no longer as cruel to her sister. She brought home B's and C's; no A's, but no D's either. There was no solid evidence that Allison was drinking alcohol, yet Phyllis found her frequent use of gum suspicious. But when Phyllis told Stuart, he accused her of looking for trouble.

Phyllis now describes Allison's behavior during the first semester at the parochial school as marginal. While Allison had not really shaped up the way they wished, both Phyllis and Stuart believed she was better—and they were all able to live with some degree of peace.

Then the moratorium ended—abruptly. Shortly after the school Christmas break, Phyllis received a call from the mother of one of Allison's classmates. The mother had returned home earlier than expected and found Allison, her own daughter, and several older boys helping themselves to alcohol from her liquor cabinet.

Phyllis was now adamant about taking different action. She had heard that a chemical dependency expert was speaking at the local high school, and she convinced Stuart to attend. After the speaker heard about Allison's behavior, she said she thought it possible that Allison was addicted to alcohol. She referred Phyllis and Stuart to me.

Although as adolescents we tested parental values and struggled toward independence, our worlds were safer and simpler than Allison's and her peers. We did not have to make life-threatening decisions about alcohol use when we were only ten years old. Nor were we exposed to the whole battery of debilitating drugs that is available to our children today.

When we were in high school, girls had to decide whether to make out or protect their reputation; boys had to plot ways to get a car and gain sexual experience. And our worlds were upwardly mobile; we were pretty sure we could do as well, if not better, than our parents. A great many of us also had access to grandparents, aunts, uncles, cousins—a whole array of family members who cared about our welfare.

The problems confronting adolescents today are much more complex. I never even heard of the word *ecology* when I was growing up. Today we have forests killed by acid rain; polluted air, rivers, and lakes; endangered species. Resources once considered infinite and invulnerable have become limited and vulnerable, as has our very planet. A recent survey of 40,000 teenagers ranked a nuclear holocaust as the number one concern of boys and the number two concern of girls, second only to their fear of the death of a parent.

Today crime infests our streets, and terrorists kill our innocent children. The United States involved itself at enormous human expense in Vietnam and shows itself capable of doing the same thing all over again in other parts of the world. We confuse the criminal behavior of elected officials with patriotism and attempt tax evasion as if it were a national pastime. And for the first time in the history of our nation, we are presenting our children with the prospect of a lower standard of living than we ourselves enjoyed.

The world of today's youth is different in other ways. The rate of separation, divorce, and remarriage has increased dramatically. Unheard of in our time, nontraditional families have proliferated: gay couples raising children together; single women having children; a divorced parent living with a lover; marriages of househusbands and career-wives; two-career marriages; voluntarily childless marriages; test-tube babies; surrogate mothers.

It is no longer considered unfeminine to run marathons or lift weights. Teenage girls can attend Harvard, Yale, Columbia, and Princeton right along with their male peers. Yet the old double standard lingers: women still receive unequal pay for equal or comparable work. Private clubs still admit few female members. We may praise female leaders of other nations, but we have yet to elect one as our president. It is true that today's women are not in the back of the bus—but neither are they all the way up front with the men. And they're definitely not driving.

The rules of sexuality have also changed. Today's teenagers have a different set of values about sex, a greater amount of knowledge, easier access to contraceptives and abortion, and fears about sexually transmitted diseases such as herpes and AIDS. While sex may be easier to come by today, it can also literally kill.

Today's youth have a far more confusing and complex array of choices than we did as adolescents. As they engage in the process of trying out new behavior and values to see what feels right, they must make decisions regarding the use of alcohol and drugs—decisions that often bear serious consequences. Whereas we had to make choices about using alcohol at ages fifteen or sixteen—when we were in high school—today's youth face these decisions in grade school, at ages nine or ten.

In 1984 a survey taken for PRIDE (Parents' Resource Institute for Drug Education) showed that 33 percent of sixth graders had tried alcohol. (By comparison, only 14 percent of high school seniors at that time had tried alcohol when they were sixth graders.) From 1983 to 1984 alcohol use by sixth graders had more than doubled. Perhaps it was because 45 percent of fifth graders reported more pressure from their peers to drink.

But the pressure to drink alcohol can even occur among younger age groups. The Metropolitan Life Insurance Company's *Statistical Bulletin* reported that of more than 500,000 U.S. school children, 26 percent of fourth graders believe that their peers are drinking alcohol, and 34 percent feel peer pressure to do so. The Gallup Youth Survey released in 1988 found that 55 percent of adolescents named drug abuse as the biggest problem facing their generation—more than double the 27 percent found in 1977, when the survey was first conducted.

The most ominous fact of all is that persons fifteen to twenty-five years of age—traditionally the healthiest members of our society—have become the most endangered. Over the last decade in the United States, the fifteen- to twenty-five-year-old age group is the only one whose death rate is increasing. At unheard-of-rates, young people are succumbing to suicides, fatal accidents, and homicides, many of which are related to an increased use of alcohol and other drugs.

Although drugs of all sorts and descriptions—from marijuana to heroin, cocaine to amphetamines, crack to such designer drugs as Ecstasy—are used in epidemic proportions throughout the United States, it is alcohol that is the drug of choice for vast numbers of adolescents. A 1989 survey conducted by the University of Michigan's Institute for Social Research found that although cocaine use had declined significantly among high school seniors nationally, alcohol use had declined only modestly. According to the social psychologist Lloyd Johnston, the prevalence of alcohol use reflects "its enculturated status in American society."

The earlier children use alcohol, the more prone they are to develop a wide range of problems, including addiction to both alcohol and other drugs. Allison, who started drinking at age ten, illustrates the pervasive, devastating effects of early alcohol use on both adolescents and their families. Allison's story also points out a common fallacy that many parents share: that children from healthy families, good schools, and stable communities do not get involved in substance abuse. As Allison's parents painfully discovered, harmful chemical involvement is no respecter of class, socioeconomic status, or quality of neighborhood. Allison had everything going for her, but she became harmfully involved with alcohol anyway. No matter how hard parents, teachers, or community leaders try, there are inevitably teenagers like Allison—healthy, normal, middle-class kids—who get hooked.

Remember, though, that the majority of today's teenagers *are* healthy. It *is* possible for children to successfully travel the road to maturation—struggling with and being helped by parents and peers, facing the challenges of today's world—and become responsible, fully functioning adults.

FOUR

Why Kids Use Alcohol and Other Drugs

Brad liked excitement; actually, he craved it. Even when very young he loved the thrills of roller coasters and daring maneuvers on his skateboard. He learned to ski jump before most kids his age had mastered skis. He liked living on the edge, and for him, chemicals were just another frontier. When he first heard about crack, he looked all over until he found some. He's pretty sure he was the first kid in his town to check it out.

Brad started smoking cigarettes and drinking alcohol when he was ten, smoked marijuana at eleven, snorted cocaine at twelve, and smoked crack at thirteen. Soon thereafter he was forcibly admitted to the adolescent unit of a psychiatric hospital.

Neither of his parents, Barbara and John, smoked, so they could readily smell tobacco smoke on Brad's clothes. Despite their efforts to get him to stop, he began to smoke cigarettes openly in front of them. When they found rolling papers in his room, they suspected marijuana, but they believed Brad when he explained that he preferred rolling his own tobacco. They knew he occasionally drank alcohol. Once they had been called by other parents to come and get him because he had passed out; another time Brad had vomited and passed out in the hedge alongside the house. But they had no idea Brad was using cocaine, much less crack. They had never even heard of crack; hardly anyone had in those days.

According to his parents, Brad had always been precocious, way ahead of his peers both physically and intellectually. He walked at eight months, talked in sentences at eleven months, read at three years, skipped fourth grade, and, when in the sixth grade, was functioning at a tenth-grade level or higher in most subjects. With little effort he got A's across the board.

Never an easy child, Brad demanded more attention than either of his siblings, and was quickly bored. With all his daring exploits, Brad was forever breaking bones. For a while Barbara felt as at home in the emergency room of the local hospital as in her own living room. Nevertheless, Barbara and John thought of Brad as a happy child, a natural extrovert and leader—cheerful, cooperative, optimistic, and full of energy.

According to John, "Everything changed by the time Brad was in the eighth grade. He'd turned into a total stranger who was impossible to control. Nothing worked, no matter what we said or did. On several occasions he stayed out all night, and once he stayed away for five days." Only much later did they learn that Brad had been on a round-the-clock crack binge, for as long as his money lasted.

Barbara recalled that Brad would be depressed or wildly euphoric, "and we'd never know why." She also reported that Brad used to blow up at the least little thing. "His rage and temper tantrums were awesome. I hate to admit this, but we were afraid of him. He threw plates, and once he chased his older sister with a butcher knife. I still shudder at the thought. Thank goodness John was home. Once our neighbor complained because Brad and his friends had torn up his newly sodded lawn with their bikes—the next day, Brad tried to set his house on fire."

"That's the first time we had him hospitalized," John explained. "He had to be dragged off in a straitjacket. It was terrible to watch, but we knew we had to do it. We'd been sending Brad to a psychiatrist for several months, but now it seemed like he'd become totally unmanageable, totally crazy.

"Brad turned overnight from a preppy to a punk. The way he dressed really got to me. He wore the same outfit every single day: long, black tails that he'd bought at some secondhand clothing store, a torn T-shirt, jeans with holes in them, and sneakers that he refused to lace. He had about five earrings going up the side of one ear, and his hair was shaved in some spots and spiked straight up in others. He looked like a damn freak!

"He was suspended from school several times that year for cutting classes. He wasn't bringing home straight A's anymore, and we got notes from his teachers telling us that Brad was not turning in his work on time, or if he did, it was incomplete. But most of the school's complaints were about his open defiance in the classroom."

"Don't forget the stealing," Barbara added.

"That's right," John said. "Brad stole money from us all the time. Barb carried her purse with her from room to room. She even kept her jewelry in her purse. In fact, he'd already hocked some of her best pieces."

Brad's behavior and emotional problems overrode any concerns Barbara and John had about his chemical use. They did not know that Brad's use of alcohol, marijuana, cocaine, and crack was the underlying cause.

A survey of some 16,000 American high school seniors conducted in 1988 by the University of Michigan's Institute of Social Research showed that one out of two students had used illicit drugs; 92 percent had used alcohol; 64 percent were current alcohol users; 35 percent were heavy drinkers, having had five or more drinks in the previous two weeks; 47 percent had used marijuana; 18 percent were current marijuana users; 12 percent had used cocaine; 3 percent were current cocaine users; 5 percent had used crack; and 1.6 percent were current crack users.

And that's the chemical use picture from "the cream of the crop"—the students who complete high school. Nationwide, approximately 15 percent are high school dropouts, of whom an estimated 90 percent are drug involved.

Since the 1960s, when the drug culture came into being, all sorts of attempts have been made to get kids to say no. Kids are *still* saying yes. Because of the variety of reasons that kids use drugs, "just saying no" doesn't always work. The solution to the drug problem in this nation requires a radical approach. Unfortunately, 94 percent of the current federal budget allocation for the war on drugs goes to supply reduction; only 6 percent goes toward reducing society's demand for drugs. The only way to solve the drug problem is to reduce the demand— and that requires educating children long before they ever arrive at the doors of elementary schools. It also requires teaching parents how to parent preventively. Until then, kids are going to say yes.

You have to remember that kids, like cats, are curious. Maturing and experimenting go hand in hand. Adolescents are drawn very naturally to those activities they associate with adulthood: drinking alcohol, experimenting with sex, driving cars, and trying out drugs. Adults may not like having their children experimenting with chemicals, but they have to be alert to the possibility of such experimentation *simply because it goes with the age*. The very nature of adolescence is to find out what things feel like.

And since the nature of adolescence involves expressions of defiance and rebellion, many kids will use drugs simply because they know their parents are against it, or because it is illegal. Using fake ID cards to obtain alcohol is a thrill to them; although getting caught may be bad news, *almost* getting caught is a real kick. You might not think it's great to have police cars with sirens wailing and lights flashing, or irate parents charging in on an underage keg party, with teenagers fleeing in all directions, but the kids will get mileage out of the story for weeks. They'll walk a little taller than the unfortunate souls who missed out, and just about every kid in the school will wish he had been there. The whole escapade may even rate space in the school yearbook!

Besides, adolescents are also drawn to chemicals because using them actually "looks" like fun. The user displays all kinds of pleasant feelings; he becomes less inhibited, more talkative, playful, daring, relaxed, or boisterous. Parents can talk about the dangers of drugs, schools can arrange for former adolescent junkies to tell kids the facts, but kids still tend to believe what they see: junkies who got away with it and their using peers having fun. How bad can something be when it looks so good?

Both advertisements and rock music invite kids to enjoy the good life by drinking beer, wine, or hard liquor or by taking other drugs. They make it clear that a life without chemicals is not worth living. At any hour of any day children can hear or see that camaraderie, every teen's wish, occurs automatically with alcohol, and that feeling wasted is a desirable or enviable state.

In past years, leaders such as John F. Kennedy and Martin Luther King, Jr., galvanized the youth of our nation. Today's galvanizers are rock musicians, movie stars, and athletes, some of whom are so stoned that they do not survive but become martyrs in death. Others go in and out of chemical dependency treatment centers with such seeming ease and in such numbers that the centers appear as innocuous as health spas—and as chic. And the life-destroying illness, chemical dependency, for which they are treated appears as insignificant—and as common—as being a few pounds overweight.

Another reason for adolescent use of alcohol and other drugs is ready availability. Teenage beer parties, which often include marijuana, are commonplace. In fact, alcohol-free parties are virtually nonexistent in many communities. It is no accident that alcohol and marijuana are the most widely used drugs; they are the most readily available.

Like Brian, many adolescents will limit their own drug use to alcohol and marijuana, no matter the availability of other drugs. Others, without such self-imposed limits, will not use other drugs simply because they are not as readily available. But now drugs of all kinds are sold in virtually every community, large or small, urban or rural. Crack, a concentrated form of cocaine, is sold in Guymon, a town of 10,000 people in the Oklahoma panhandle, just as it is in New York City.

Toni considers herself lucky. The number of girls in her high school class was far greater than the number of boys, "and it was mostly the boys who did drugs. We knew they were doing coke and acid and stuff, but they didn't do it in front of us, and they certainly didn't offer it to us. They probably didn't have enough to go around. I would've had to ask for it, and I just wasn't prepared to do that. In college coke is all over the place, and I took some once at a party. Coke felt sooooo fantastic! I mean, I was flying, soaring; I could've taken on the whole world. The next day all I could think about was how to get more cocaine. That really scared me. I actually called my mom to tell her I had to come home that weekend. When I told my mom what had happened, she said the same thing had happened to her. She'd been given cocaine once when she had her sinuses treated and said that even though it was raining, the whole world seemed sunny. She even felt bad about herself for a while because she kept hoping her sinus problems would return so she could get more cocaine. Just talking about it with my mom made it manageable. I felt I didn't have to take it again just because I wanted it. Now that I look back upon it, I'm glad that happened when I was nineteen and not fifteen. No way could I have handled cocaine then. The high was too great. But I'm glad in a way that it happened, because now I have a respect for drugs that I never really had before. Now I make sure I keep my distance.''

Adolescents do not like to have people think that they use chemicals as a result of peer pressure, and they are quick to deny any such influence. ''No one poured it down my throat.'' ''No one ever ridiculed me for saying no.'' ''Drugs were there, but no one forced them.'' ''No one's making me drink.'' ''I don't have to use if I don't want to.'' But a closer look shows that insidious pressure is, in fact, a reality and that its impact is enormous.

Most adolescents drink alcohol, considering it normal behavior. Close to one-fourth smoke marijuana regularly. Over half have tried other illicit drugs. The fact is that what in our day would have been considered aberrant behavior—adolescent chemical use—has become normal in our children's day. What we would have been ostracized for doing, our children are ostracized for not doing. What we would have been afraid to try, our children are afraid not to.

Another reason adolescents use alcohol and other drugs is that many adults do not take such chemical use seriously. Not taking it seriously takes many forms: denying that chemical use occurs; regarding drug use as a phase kids inevitably go through; feeling uncomfortable confronting a teenager who is suspected of using; feeling unsure of what to do about an adolescent user and therefore doing nothing; and worst of all, condoning such behavior.

Conversely, when adults do take chemical use seriously, so do their children. Unfortunately, because alcohol use is as much a part of the American fabric as Thanksgiving, the Super Bowl, and the Fourth of July, many parents who regard other drugs with proper respect do not consider adolescent consumption of beer, wine coolers, and other alcoholic beverages problematic.

Alcohol kills more children than all other drugs combined. Yet I still meet parents who are grateful that their child only drinks alcohol and is not using marijuana or other drugs. Some parents take tolerance of alcohol use to illegal extremes by actually purchasing kegs of beer for their kids. Others believe supervised drinking is a safe solution, so they watch their children drink, or drink with them. Others attempt to walk a precarious line between tolerance and restraint, and seem afraid to take a solid stand on no alcohol use. What these parents don't realize is that alcohol is a drug—a very potent one.

Yet another reason adolescents use alcohol and other drugs is because it feels good. All the chemicals kids use—including alcohol in any form, marijuana, hashish, inhalants, cocaine in any form, Valium, Quaaludes, LSD, peyote, mescaline, heroin, Ecstasy—cause euphoria, a heightened state of being, to one degree or another. Think pleasure, not pain, if you want to get a handle on adolescent chemical use. Kids may already be feeling good, but the chemical will make them feel better.

Bill was angry, very angry, the day he brought his son, Mark, in for a chemical dependency evaluation. He had just picked up Mark from school, where the boy had been caught smoking marijuana. "This isn't the first time. Mark's already been expelled from one school for smoking pot," Bill raged. "Last month they suspended him for smoking . . . he's only been back two weeks and they've caught him again. This kid's not stupid; he tests in the top percentile. So something else is going on, and I want to get to the bottom of it."

Mark looked miserable and I could see why. Bill seemed to exude power from every pore. I was not at all surprised to learn he was the CEO of a large corporation. Mark was quite a contrast: a cute, soft-spoken, laid-back seventeen-year-old, hidden behind lots of long hair, baggy clothes, high top sneakers, and dangling laces.

But more than anger and fear was present between these

two. Even when angry, Bill was looking upon his son with love, not the scorn or disgust I see on the faces of many parents. And Mark lacked the defiance one might expect in this situation. Instead, he looked sad, incredibly sad. There was some kind of special bonding here—that much was clear.

Their story, as it unfolded, did in fact reveal a close relationship. Bill was not only powerful, he was also sensitive. And so was Mark. They had been through a lot together, both good and bad.

Mark's mother, Arlene, had died of cancer when he was twelve. Bill obtained a leave of absence for more than a year during the period before and after his wife's death, wanting to be with Arlene and Mark, their only child. During this time, Bill and Mark gave each other all the comfort they could.

After Arlene's death, Bill and Mark, both natural athletes, traveled for several weeks, backpacking through the Sangre de Cristo mountains in Colorado and whitewater rafting in British Columbia. "We wanted to be together," Bill explained, "but alone. We wanted some personal challenge. I guess when you get down to it, we wanted to work out our grief physically in places where we'd feel close to God . . . and close to each other. Please, please help us," he asked softly as tears welled up. "Now I feel like I'm losing my son, and that's more than I'm going to be able to handle."

Upon returning home the fall after their trip, much of their grief had been resolved and both felt ready to get on with their lives. They lived together in an apartment in New York City with Eva, their longtime housekeeper. Mark returned to school and Bill to his company. Their lives went along smoothly until about a year ago.

Bill reports that Mark started to withdraw around his sixteenth birthday. Instead of sharing his experiences with his father as he had in the past, Mark started spending a lot of time alone in his room. His grades began to fall, and he seemed to lose his former ambition. He no longer jogged each morning, and he spent less and less time with his former friends.

Eva told Bill that Mark began to sleep for several hours after school and that his eyes often looked red. Mark went out on weekends, always keeping his curfews, but Bill never knew where he went or with whom. Several times Mark came home drunk from an evening out. Once he was so drunk that he vomited in the hallway and passed out in his own puke. "I checked to see that he was breathing okay, then just left him there," Bill reported.

A specimen of physical fitness, Bill worked out every morning, jogged several miles on weekends, did not use drugs of any kind, and drank only an occasional glass of wine. Bill let Mark know in no uncertain terms that he did not want him using alcohol and other drugs. If he found evidence of drinking, he would ground Mark the following weekend. And each time Mark would promise not to drink again in the future.

Bill had never seen any evidence of marijuana use, nor had Eva ever found any stashes or paraphernalia while cleaning his room, so Bill was shocked the first time Mark was suspended from school for smoking marijuana. "Now I can see I shouldn't have been so surprised. Eva had been telling me for some time that Mark's eyes were often red. I really don't know why I let that pass like I did."

Bill reported that he also had become increasingly concerned about Mark's mood over the past year. "Mark seems sad a lot, like he had been when his mother was dying," he said. Yet when Bill offered help or opportunities for Mark to talk, Mark would claim there was nothing wrong. For quite some time Bill had also noticed a new sullenness about Mark, as if he were not only sad, but angry as well. "He's been giving me a lot of surly retorts, and that's not like Mark at all. We'd always bantered with each other, but now there's a viciousness creeping in that's never been there before."

In his private sessions with me, Mark revealed a pattern of chemical use that was progressive and out of control. He had started drinking alcohol at friends' homes shortly after he turned fifteen. Initially his use involved beer two or three times a month. Now he was drinking hard liquor every weekend night, and two to three cans of beer at lunch every day during the week. He had started smoking marijuana a few months before his sixteenth birthday. For a short period, he would have a "joint or two" two or three times a week; now he said he was smoking "pretty much around the clock. Dope and booze! Some life, huh?"

Mark admitted he had tried to stop many times but couldn't. "A few months ago, after I'd gotten kicked out of my other school, I stopped doing dope for a week, but I couldn't stop the booze. Other times, I've gone without booze but would do dope. At no time have I been able to give up both. I'm hooked. I know I'm hooked. I don't need you to tell me that.

"You know what else? I have blackouts, lots of them, all the time. Most days I can't even recall how I get home from school. I don't even remember being suspended last month. They tell me I met with the headmaster, and I'm sure I did, but I've got news: I don't remember it. Not that I want to remember it, you understand; I'm having enough trouble dealing with the stuff I do remember."

It appeared that Mark had reached the end of his rope—his addiction rope, that is. "I can't go on like this. I've got to get some help." More than anything, he said he could not stand losing his father's love. "The booze and dope have come between us. Please, can you help? I want to get him back . . . and I want to get me back."

Recalling the early days of his chemical use, Mark said, "I loved alcohol and pot when I first started. They made me feel great. I don't think I was feeling bad—I mean, I missed my mom, but, you know, I was pretty much over that and really liked my life. Watching her die was the worst, and I wasn't even using anything then, so I don't really think I started using because I felt down. I started using because that's what one did. I continued using 'cause I liked being up, way up.

"I don't get those highs anymore. Now when I use, it's so I can feel normal, or halfway normal. You know, it's strange, but I miss my mom more now than ever. When things were good, I didn't miss her so much. But now they're not so good, and I miss her a lot," Mark confessed, tears flowing freely down his cheeks.

Adults tend to lose sight of the pleasure associated with adolescent chemical use. They assume kids are having problems and that's why they use. Some kids do use chemicals to mask pain, *but most use chemicals to increase pleasure*. It is only later, after a harmful involvement with chemicals has developed—which by itself causes all kinds of problems and emotional pain—that teenagers use chemicals as a means of escape. Then, as Mark described, they use in order to feel normal.

But it is true that a minority of adolescents use chemicals initially to cope with the pain of their lives. These kids often go at chemical use with a vengeance, as if they are about to self-destruct. On closer inspection, their motive is often revealed: it's the desire to strike out at their worlds, to get even. These kids are heartbreakers for those of us in the addiction field. Often they have parents who neglect or abandon them, who just don't seem to care about them, or who abuse them.

Kimberly stopped by to see me a few weeks ago. She does that from time to time, but I dread her visits. Each time I think she can't get much worse and still live. But each time I'm relieved to know she is still alive.

As usual she looked terrible. She was adorned, if that's the word, entirely in black. Black scruffy boots; black, impossibly short miniskirt; black shirt; short hair with light brown roots showing through the black; bruises near her right ear and on several fingers of her left hand; grayish dirt ingrained on her neck and hands. But this time, even though as thin as ever, she was bloated. The areas around her nose, eyes, and lips were swollen and red, looking sore to the touch. Her right wrist and part of her right hand were encased in a dirty, frayed bandage.

"What happened?" I wondered.

"The ether just went thruuumph, blew up all over the place. It happens, you know."

"Freebasing?"

"What else?" she answered.

No kid starts out like this. In fact, until she was fifteen, Kimberly was a super-good kid—super-good trying desperately to make up for super-bad parents. She was pretty in the pictures she once showed me. A bubbly, junior varsity cheerleader in one, a serious student in another, a smiling kid with lots of friends in still another. She got good grades, took good care of the house for her drunk mother, shopped and cooked for her drunk father, and went to church regularly. She even handled all the arrangements for her own confirmation, despite her fear that one or both of her parents might refuse to come at the last minute, or that they would attend while embarrassingly intoxicated.

Then she stopped being good. Just before her fifteenth birthday, her father left, saying he wanted a divorce. Then her mother, though she got a job as a waitress to help support them, started disappearing—first one night at a time, then days at a time. And Kimberly gave up.

Her parents had neglected her terribly and had abused her both verbally and physically. Still, Kimberly needed them. Without them, she had no one to care for and felt she no longer had any value—"like I was nothing." She also felt scared, totally abandoned, and ashamed. She believed that if her friends knew what was going on in her family, they also would abandon her. So she abandoned them and joined the drug-using crowd. "I knew they'd accept me."

At first, Kimberly only drank alcohol. "But the pressure was on. I knew if I was going to hang around with them, I'd have to be like them, all the way. So I took the crack they gave, and it blew me away. The feeling was so intense, so fantastic. I smoked it and smoked it and smoked it. Nothing else mattered but that feeling . . . and getting more crack. The second time I used it a bunch of us went to a crack house in the city, and I went on a three-day binge, staying until my money ran out. Then they threw me out in the street like a piece of garbage. I didn't know where to go. I thought of calling one of my parents and reversing the charges, but I didn't think they'd accept my call. Then I remembered Covenant House, a place I'd read about that rescues kids. So I looked up their address in a phone book and worked my way over there. After a couple of days they tracked down my dad—they never did find my mom—and he came to get me. He wasn't drunk, but he was in a rage. He told me if he ever got called to rescue me again like that, he'd beat the shit out of me. And then he slapped me around—I guess to show me he could beat the shit out of me. And all I wanted was more crack."

A couple of years ago I thought we had a chance. For several months after Kimberly's seventeenth birthday, her mother stopped drinking and joined Alcoholics Anonymous, and both she and Kimberly started working with me on a regular basis. Her mother quickly picked up some badly needed parenting skills, and Kimberly started to respond.

At that time, Kimberly was earning money for crack by hooking over at the railroad station and clearly hated her addiction— at least the crashes, the terrible comedowns after each use, when she literally wanted to die. "I'd dream of death, how good it'd feel to be out of it all." By then, she had also had three abortions. But she wasn't quite ready to give up her addiction. Finally, after several sessions and some loving parenting from a sober mother, Kimberly told me that the reason she was refusing to go to a treatment center was that she was afraid she had AIDS, "so why bother." After a few more sessions, she agreed to be tested. The day the tests came back negative, she entered a drug treatment center—hopeful for the first time in years.

Then, once again, her world fell apart. First, her boyfriend, a crack user, committed suicide. Then, on visiting day, her mother arrived drunk at the treatment center. That night Kimberly ran away. Since then she's evaded several attempts by the Department of Social Services to help her, even though she does show up at their various shelters from time to time—and at my office.

Kimberly never had the opportunity to live a normal life. Unlike most adolescents, her entry into chemical use had nothing to do with pleasure. It had to do with revenge.

What children learn as they experiment with chemicals is astounding. First, they learn that the beer, marijuana, or whatever really does make them feel good. Then, with repeated use, they learn that the chemical always works. Each time they use it they experience a change in their mood in a welcome direction—a high. It is not long before they learn they can trust the chemical absolutely. The chemical, in fact, can easily and quickly become the only thing in their lives that seems worthy of absolute trust. Nothing else is guaranteed to make them feel good. Next, after playing around with amounts and combinations—two six-packs rather than three cans, for example, or beer plus marijuana, or alcohol plus cocaine—children learn they can control their degree of euphoria. They can get a buzz on or blot out totally. They feel in control; they can make the chemicals do whatever they wish.

How children learn about chemicals is also astounding. Adolescents learn all this by *doing*—the most potent form of education. It is no wonder the important factual information children receive about alcohol and other drugs in health classes or from their parents so often is ignored. Attempting to address a feeling experience through intellect alone is an exercise in futility.

Children know chemicals feel good. They do not *think* it; they *know* it. Their experiences with chemicals prove to them time and time again that, without any effort, they can feel great immediately by simply using a chemical which they trust totally and over which they have great power. Is that reality? Not by a long shot. There is, in fact, nothing in life that matches the power of alcohol and other drugs.

Adolescents I work with frequently ask, "What've you got that's as good?" My answer is simple: "Nothing." What can I say? Even if I come up with something exciting, like winning a tennis match, making high honors, writing a poem, I would hear in return, "What if I lose?" "That's work." "That'll take forever."

To sum it all up, adolescents use alcohol and other drugs for a multitude of reasons—because they want to find out what it feels like; because it is exciting and looks like fun; because they have been seduced by advertisements and chemical-using role models; because chemicals are readily available; because chemical use is "in" and may be tacitly condoned by parents; and because alcohol and other drugs are virtually guaranteed to give them an immediate high with little effort. A few adolescents, like Kimberly, use chemicals to diminish the pain in their lives. Most, like Toni, Brian, Ricky, Allison, Brad, and Mark, use chemicals, at least initially, to enhance the pleasure of their lives.

Drugs of Choice

What do you know about crack, Ecstasy, dope, smack, ice, Rush, and Locker Room? Are you aware that each of these slang terms denotes a highly potent, addictive drug commonly used among adolescents today? The more you know about what drugs kids use—and how those drugs affect adolescents— the better you can do your job of preventive parenting, or of intervening skillfully in a chemical-use situation. Despite the wealth of facts about drugs flooding today's news, a variety of misleading myths still dominate our awareness of adolescent chemical use.

For example, cocaine (and its powerful derivative, crack) is currently *the* high-visibility drug in the United States. It deserves visibility: it's deadly. But cocaine does not kill nearly as many Americans each year as alcohol.

It may surprise you that alcohol kills far more people than all other drugs combined (excluding tobacco). It is our leading drug killer. According to Dr. David E. Smith, an expert in the area of chemical dependency, over 100,000 people die each year in the United States as a result of problems associated with alcohol use.

Sixty-four percent of high school seniors are current users

of alcohol, and 21 percent are current users of illicit drugs. What these figures show is that more kids use alcohol than all other drugs combined. What the figures do not show is the fact that, for the most part, the kids who use alcohol are the same kids who use other drugs.

Because alcohol is widely accepted as part of America's social fabric, it is usually the first drug used by adolescents. Its social acceptability and ready availability make it not only the leading drug killer among young people, but also a gateway drug—one that leads to the use of other drugs.

A central nervous system depressant, alcohol releases inhibitions within the cerebral cortex of the brain and causes a sense of euphoria. As it alters the brain's processes, it in turn affects our thought processes, feelings, and behavior. No mood-altering, mind-changing drug can be considered safe for children who are still in the process of intellectual and emotional maturation.

Additionally, alcohol destroys cells. Most people now know that alcohol can cause birth defects and contribute to an increased incidence of breast cancer, as well as to destruction of the liver. But few seem to know that alcohol can damage other vital organs, including the brain—a destruction that is visible upon autopsy. Not even heroin, our most stigmatized drug, is so devastating.

Ten-, eleven-, and twelve-year-old children, a larger number of whom are now beginning to drink alcohol, are still growing physically. Their bodies, including their brains and internal organs, are still developing. One can only speculate as to the harmful effects such a cellular-destructive drug can have on a body that has not even begun to reach physical maturity.

A twelve-ounce can of beer, a four-and-one-half-ounce glass of wine, and one ounce of hard liquor all contain the same amount of alcohol. Budding adolescents are not known to do things in moderation. In fact, in their early experimental years they often drink to get drunk, stopping only when they are too sick or too intoxicated to drink further. Eleven-year-old children can consume a six-pack of beer in very short order, but many adults remain undisturbed when this occurs; they do not seem to realize that one six-pack of beer has the same impact as three double martinis.

Adolescents who use alcohol are more prone to develop alcoholism than are adults. In fact, the earlier the use, the higher the incidence of addiction. It is also known that adolescents telescope alcoholism. While it takes an adult anywhere from five to twenty years to progress to late-stage alcohol addiction, adolescents can reach the late stage in anywhere from six months to three years. Once addicted, adolescents are harder to treat than adults for a number of reasons, not the least of which is that they do not have a history of mature life experiences to fall back on as resources for recovery.

And what will happen to the increasing numbers of pre-adolescent drinkers, the ten- and eleven-year-olds? The data available indicates that the addiction rate of these youngsters will be even higher. Their disease process is likely to be extremely rapid, and consequently more violent. Furthermore, their recoveries are bound to be very difficult to achieve. They will not even have adolescent maturation to fall back on, much less the mature life experiences of adults.

Until the 1980s, relatively few preadolescents used alcohol on any kind of regular basis; but from observing those who have, it is clear that alcohol can readily abort maturation. Even if they escape alcohol addiction, they do not mature along normal routes. As they enter their teens, they escalate their alcohol use to dangerous levels, abuse or develop addiction to other drugs, show deviant or criminal behavior, and function poorly at school and at home. If they survive their adolescence, and many do not, they tend to become delinquent, marginally functional adults, unable to accept responsibility for their own behavior. Often they appear on the welfare rolls, are incarcerated in hospitals or jails, join the growing ranks of the homeless, or become totally dependent on their parents. To say the least, regular alcohol use by preadolescents does not paint a pretty picture.

Over the past decade, the whole process of alcohol experimentation followed by regular use has gradually filtered down to an ever-younger age group, so that today one-third of sixth graders are experimenting with alcohol. Will this earlier experimental use of alcohol result in an earlier regular use of alcohol? The chances are it will. If so, for the first time in our history, large numbers of children will be using a drug capable of thwarting adolescent development before that development has even begun. The resulting toll on these youngsters, their families, and our society will be staggering.

Although the use of tobacco by adolescents is outside the scope of this book, as parents you should be aware of its significance as a gateway drug. Like its companion drug, alcohol, tobacco is considered by many parents to be ''safe,'' different from ''unsafe'' drugs like marijuana, cocaine, and heroin. Ironically, *social acceptance is not equivalent to safety*. Alcohol and tobacco are gateway drugs, because those adolescents who do not use either one tend not to use any other drugs. Defenders of alcohol and tobacco use are fond of pointing out that not all drinkers and smokers become users of other drugs. This contention is beside the point; virtually all adolescent drug users begin their drug careers with alcohol and frequently with cigarettes.

It is unclear whether most chemically dependent young people begin using alcohol or tobacco first. What is clear is that while not all drinkers smoke, nearly all adolescent smokers drink. Clearer still is the evidence that the use of one or both of these drugs seems to offer many adolescents the permission to use other drugs.

Second only to alcohol use in its prevalence among adolescents, tobacco use stimulates the central nervous system much as cocaine. As the nicotine causes the heart to beat faster, it creates a surge of energy and a sense of alertness and clearheadedness. Although it is not immediately life-threatening, tobacco use on a sustained basis causes lung cancer and contributes to emphysema, asthma, and other serious bronchial diseases. It also causes heart disease and low birth weight. Over 300,000 Americans die each year as a result of maladies associated with cigarette smoking.

Neither alcohol nor tobacco carries the stigma associated with illicit drugs, yet if parents want their kids to avoid the drugs that concern them the most, they will have to help their children avoid the least alarming drugs as well.

The third most commonly used drug is marijuana—variously called dope, pot, weed, and reefer. It is a hallucinogen that creates a sense of heightened consciousness and a state of euphoria. If you are not familiar with marijuana's appearance, imagine oregano and sage rolled into a handmade cigarette. Although usually smoked, the small seeds, stems, and leaves that form marijuana can be added to cookie batter and eaten. With its legacy of peace and counterculture connotations from the sixties, marijuana has often been considered a relatively benign drug. The marijuana of today, however, generally contains more than twice as much THC (the drug's primary psychoactive ingredient) as that in the sixties, doubling its potency and its numerous side effects.

Marijuana causes virtually all the same problems as alcohol and tobacco, as well as a variety of additional toxic short- and long-term effects. The common perception of marijuana as physically safer than cigarettes has been proven false by recent research. Findings indicate the presence of more cancer-producing agents in marijuana smoke than in cigarette smoke. In addition, marijuana users retain the smoke in their lungs for longer periods of time to increase their high, causing greater bronchial and lung damage. One study at the UCLA School of Medicine found that the heavy deposits of carcinogens in marijuana smokers' lungs put them at exceptionally high risk of developing lung cancer.

Research in the area of the body's cellular response to marijuana has also revealed that THC (delta-9-tetrahydro-cannabinol) directly affects the human immune system by impairing a component of the white blood cell defense system, placing the user at risk for all sorts of illnesses. Also, because marijuana has been found to lower hormone levels in adolescents, normal sexual development in both boys and girls is often arrested.

In addition to the short-term effects of lowered body temperature, increased hunger (known as the munchies), rapid heart beat (up to 50 percent faster), and dry nasal passages, long-range effects are caused in part by the fact that THC remains in the body for up to thirty days. With repeated use, THC accumulates and is stored for months in the fat cells of the brain, liver, and reproductive organs.

Marijuana not only impairs adolescents physically, it also affects their emotional and intellectual faculties. The drug alters a youngster's ability to concentrate, to perceive clearly, and to be motivated for success. Perhaps the best-known side effect of THC is a state called amotivational syndrome, which is associated with chronic marijuana use. This syndrome is characterized by apathy, listlessness, lack of interest in personal appearance, and an inability to be goal-directed. This loss of energy impairs daily functioning. Although it can take several months, a year, or longer to rid the body of THC, amotivational syndrome *is* reversible if adolescents stop smoking this drug.

The fourth most commonly used drugs are the inhalants. Kids inhale fumes from aerosol cans (like whipped cream or spray paint containers); glues; gasoline; lighter, cleaning, and correction fluids; and butyl nitrite (a yellowish liquid usually sold in small bottles, often marketed in smoke shops or novelty stores under the names Rush and Locker Room). These substances cause instant rushes of euphoria, a feeling of disorientation, and a sense of weightlessness. These apparently harmless substances—all of which are legal in the United States—are actually extremely dangerous. They destroy brain cells and impair the central nervous system. Approximately half of the habitual users of inhalants suffer some degree of brain damage. Signs of inhalant use include fatigue, loss of appetite, weight loss, frequent coughing and nosebleeds, and jumbled speech.

Usually inhalants are not the primary drugs of choice for teenagers. Rather, they are more like icing on the cake, a topping for drugs such as alcohol and marijuana. However, inhalants sometimes are the primary drugs of choice for preteens—perhaps because they are readily available and easily hidden. I have known children as young as seven years old to be repeatedly sniffing the fumes from correction fluid taken from Dad's desk, or from little brown bottles of butyl nitrite from the local tobacco shop—all while Mom was cooking dinner in the kitchen.

Unlike inhalants, which depress the central nervous system, stimulants excite it, increasing blood pressure and pulse rate, motivating the body to perform at a higher level of activity, and creating feelings of exhilaration. Common side effects are insomnia, agitation, and loss of appetite. Stimulants include a wide range of drugs, from illegal substances like cocaine and crack sold on the street (through the drug trade), to amphetamines commonly available by prescription or on the street, to caffeine pills sold over the counter.

Among the more popular amphetamines are Benzedrine, Dexedrine, Sanorex, and Voranil. Usually ingested in tablet or capsule form, these drugs can also be inhaled or injected. Youngsters often start using these drugs, known as speed or uppers, to control drowsiness while studying for exams or to generate more energy before a sports event. In addition to producing immediate effects of increased energy and exhilaration, amphetamines also cause devastating long-range physical and psychological effects. Chronic abusers may experience symptoms of psychosis, including paranoia, hallucinations, and violent behavior.

The most dangerous of all the stimulants is cocaine, with its powerful derivative, crack. Made from the leaves of the coca plant, cocaine is usually sold in its water-soluble form, as a white, odorless, crystalline powder. In this form it is commonly snorted (absorbed through the mucous membranes of the nose), rubbed on the gums, or injected directly into the veins. The powder can also be smoked, swallowed, or dissolved in water and inserted deeper into the nose with an eyedropper.

A "line" or "hit" of cocaine refers to a strip about two inches long and one-quarter-inch wide, lined on a piece of glass or a mirror, then sniffed through a short straw or rolled-up dollar bill. Some adolescents have one long fingernail or a small coke spoon (often worn on a necklace) for snorting a hit of this drug. At about two dollars a hit, cocaine, once enormously expensive, has become affordable to virtually everyone. Cocaine's currently modest price has spread its use throughout all socioeconomic groups, making it readily available to adolescents across the United States.

Cocaine produces a rapid and powerful sense of euphoria. Neuroscientists have discovered that dopamine, a chemical active within the brain, is responsible for promoting feelings of pleasure. Cocaine acts in such a way as to flood the neurons with dopamine, thus creating rhapsodic feelings of pleasure that last from ten to twenty minutes. The craving to reexperience this intense pleasure is powerful, and the depression that follows the high is profound. On the average, both physical and psychological addiction is developed by an adolescent cocaine user in approximately sixteen months.

In the last decade, fatalities related to cocaine ingestion have tripled. Death can occur through respiratory failure, when the brain ceases to maintain the autonomic nervous system's functions; through cerebral hemorrhages, when a rapidly rising blood pressure bursts blood vessels in the brain; through convulsions; or through heart fibrillations, which lead to cardiac arrest. In addition, when used on a regular basis, cocaine can severely disrupt mental processes, causing such psychotic reactions as hallucination, paranoia, and violent behavior.

Signs of cocaine use include a perpetually runny nose, a chronic sore throat, nosebleeds, inflamed sinuses, holes in the nasal cartilage, hepatitis, and lung damage.

Cocaine use is not a recent phenomenon. Used as far back in history as the time of the Incan empire, the drug has been praised for its euphoria-producing properties by such notables as Sigmund Freud. Only recently have researchers become aware of the devastating effects of chronic use. Cocaine use reached epidemic proportions in the 1980s because its stimulating properties fit in with the prevailing emphasis on action, mastery, power, energy, and control. Unlike marijuana and alcohol, which reduce motivation and drive, cocaine matches the high-performance ethnic of the "me" generation.

■   ■

More highly addictive than any other drug available in the United States today is crack, the fast food of drugs. Crack, a free based form of cocaine, is made through a process in which cocaine powder is mixed with ether or baking soda, various chemical activators, and water, then heated. The resulting paste hardens and is cut into pellets resembling soap chips. It is then smoked either in cigarette form (together with tobacco or marijuana) or through a water pipe. It reaches the brain in approximately seven seconds, producing a rush of euphoria that lasts about twenty minutes and is about five to ten times as intense as that of cocaine. The term *crack* describes the sound made by the pellets as they burn.

Because crack provides the fastest known delivery of the most intense high, it has a greater addictive potential than any other drug. The greater and faster the euphoria, the greater the addiction potential for the greatest number of people. According to New York psychopharmacologist Dr. Arnold Washton, crack is currently the most addictive substance in existence. Because of its extreme potency, crack causes more physical and psychological devastation, and more violent behavior, than cocaine. Crack is sold in small glass vials with brightly colored plastic tops, usually in $5 (two pellets) and $10 (four pellets) sizes.

Although crack has been seen as epidemic primarily within inner-city neighborhoods, recently doctors, chemical dependency counselors, and crack addicts themselves have been reporting a high rate of addiction among middle-class Americans. Dr. Washton's research points to the existence of more addicts in the middle class than in any other portion of the population. Thus, contrary to popular belief, adolescents from suburban neighborhoods are at high risk to become crack addicts—as much as, if not more than, inner-city youths.

■ ■

Heroin (also known as junk, smack, horse, and dope), a semi-synthetic derivative of morphine, is an odorless, bitter-tasting white powder that is soluble in water. Most users inject heroin directly into their veins, usually through the arms and groin, causing "tracks" or scarring, although heroin can also be smoked or sniffed.

Heroin is a central nervous system depressant and produces a three- to six-hour euphoria characterized by an initial intense high followed by a state of pleasant well-being. Because of its depressant effect, users often look sluggish and, if left alone, tend to "nod out." Heroin is highly addictive and deadly. It provides a lot of pleasurable mileage for most users and quickly becomes their primary drug of choice. With repeated use, addiction occurs within a couple of weeks. Heroin interferes with the user's ability to function and in many cases causes convulsions, coma, and even death.

The rate of heroin use remained fairly constant for over twenty years but is currently on the increase, especially among cocaine users. As a stimulant, cocaine can leave the user with a severe form of agitation, which can be reduced with the use of heroin, a depressant and painkiller. Also, when combined with cocaine, heroin can create an exaggerated sense of euphoria. In the past, less than 1 percent of high school seniors used heroin. With the increase of cocaine use among adolescents and young adults, we can now expect to see an associated increase in heroin use as well.

Approximately 5 percent of today's students are current users of drugs we have not yet mentioned: narcotics other than heroin, such as codeine, morphine, Dilaudid, paregoric, Demerol, and Percodan; hallucinogens other than marijuana, such as LSD (acid), PCP (angel dust), mescaline, and mushrooms (psilocybin); sedatives such as chloral hydrate, Noctec, Somnos, Nembutal, Seconal, and Quaalude; tranquilizers such as

Valium and Miltown; and the new, so-called designer drugs, such as Ecstasy, China White, and ice.

Rarely do any of these drugs become the primary drugs of choice for adolescents. Rather, they are used on occasion as a special treat, or in conjunction with alcohol or marijuana. PCP, sedatives, and tranquilizers can exacerbate the depressant effects of alcohol and heroin, causing death or irreversible coma. Cocaine, on the other hand, wards off the intoxicating effects of alcohol and heroin, allowing one to drink more or to inject larger doses of heroin. Its effect is short-term, however, and can cause a seemingly sober drinker or heroin user to become quickly, and often dangerously, intoxicated—sometimes to the point of a fatal overdose. John Belushi, star of "Saturday Night Live," died as a result of "speedballing," that is, injecting a mixture of cocaine and heroin.

The popularity of most of these occasional-use drugs appears to be on the decline, except for the new designer drugs, whose use seems to be on the increase, particularly among college students. These synthetic designer drugs, manufactured in clandestine laboratories from readily available chemicals, cost little to produce and are many times stronger than cocaine or heroin. A current favorite, MDMA, better known as Ecstasy, offers the euphoric rush of cocaine and some of the mind-expanding qualities of the hallucinogic drug LSD. China White, a form of Fentanyl, an analgesic widely used during prolonged surgery, is 1,000 to 2,000 times stronger than heroin. A new designer drug, methamphetamine, has recently become popular in western states and appears to be gaining national momentum. A smokable, fast-acting stimulant known as ice, methamphetamine has reportedly been responsible for an increase in emergency room treatments and deaths on the West Coast.

Underground laboratories do not have strict quality control. A few years ago, a defective batch of a designer drug called

MPTP left scores of users suffering from symptoms of Parkinson's disease. Yet even if manufactured to correct specifications, these designer drugs cannot be considered safe.

Researchers have discovered that Ecstasy produces damage to the brain cells of animals, even in low doses, and it has been declared illegal in European countries. Although additional research is needed to determine why and how these designer drugs cause damage, it is now clear that they are not the harmless substances they once were believed to be.

Although we cannot predict exactly how any one person will react to a specific drug, we do know that when an individual experiences a significant degree of euphoria, he will be tempted to repeat the experience and will then be at increased risk of addiction. All of the mood-altering, mind-changing drugs discussed here are potentially addictive, some more so than others.

Alcohol and marijuana cause a mild euphoria for most users, intense euphoria for some. Those who get the most euphoric mileage will be the ones most likely to become addicted to alcohol and marijuana.

Nicotine causes only a mild euphoria but is chemically a highly addictive agent. So is heroin, which usually produces a high euphoria. Most users become addicted to nicotine and heroin, no matter the degree of euphoric experience.

Cocaine, crack, and the designer drugs cause an inordinately high euphoria for most users, and so are hard to resist. Crack, in particular, is virtually impossible to resist. Addiction can occur within a few weeks.

Let's look at how the drugs of choice affected the adolescents in our case histories so far.

Toni didn't like marijuana. "Feeling weird" was not for her, so she was not tempted to pursue pot. She reported that alcohol was only okay. But, like most people, she loved the euphoria of cocaine and had to force herself to resist it.

Brian said that although he liked alcohol, he *loved* marijuana. Marijuana gave him much more euphoric mileage. Therefore, until his father brought his use to a halt, marijuana was his drug of choice.

While heroin will quickly hook most repeat users, many users do not return for more because they find the accompanying sluggishness unpleasant. Others, like Ricky, love heroin and become addicted within months, if not weeks. Not only do they experience a strong sense of euphoria, but they enjoy its mellowing quality.

Allison is unusual. She claims not to have tried any drug other than alcohol. She was proud of her ability to get a lot of euphoric mileage out of alcohol and to drink large amounts without becoming intoxicated. She said she never felt a need for other drugs; besides, she was afraid to try.

Brad was prepared to try any and all drugs. In cocaine he found the one that fulfilled his need for excitement. While he did not like the enervating qualities of either alcohol or marijuana, he did like combining alcohol with cocaine. On many occasions he became grossly intoxicated once the effects from the cocaine had worn off and would have to be carted home by friends, or occasionally by the police.

"That's what finally did it for us, all those police officers," his father reported. "Brad had been admitted to the psychiatric hospital three times. He was placed in a school for emotionally disturbed adolescents for most of one year, and he had been seeing a psychiatrist for close to three years. But things were getting worse, not better. When the police started bringing him home intoxicated, we began to realize we should be doing something about his drinking."

"I know it sounds stupid that it took us so long to get the idea," his mother, Barbara, admitted. "After all, we saw him drunk a lot. We also suspected he was using cocaine because he wore a little gold spoon around his neck, and once I found a water pipe in his room which later we discovered was for smoking crack—not that we knew what crack was about. But we were so caught up in all his emotional problems that we kept thinking if we could get those resolved, he'd cut down on the drinking and drugs. Once we started going to Al-Anon because of our concerns about his drinking, we could see that we had it all turned around, that his drinking and drugging were the cause of his emotional problems. It kills me to think we wasted years of his life. They were years of anguish for all of us.''

Like so many parents, Barbara had the cause-effect relationship backwards. Instead of seeing that chemical dependency creates emotional illness, many mothers and fathers believe that psychological problems are causing the disruptive, chemical-abusing behavior. This erroneous thinking wastes precious health, time, and energy, delaying diagnosis, intervention, and treatment.

Mark said he tried every drug out there at least once, except for heroin and crack. ''The word was out on those. I knew if I tried them, I wouldn't be able to stop.'' He said that once when he and his father were home alone, he came upon some acid (LSD) that he had forgotten about—and took it. ''Too much! I broke all the rules. I had no one with me to keep me in touch with reality. And it was a baaaaad trip. The walls were moving in on me—the ceiling, too. I crawled under my bed to protect myself. I wanted to scream, but somewhere in the back of my mind I knew I couldn't. I knew I had to keep my dad from knowing I was tripping. And then it seemed like I was screaming. So I gagged myself. God! It was terrible. It took hours to get back down.''

Mark also said he never was crazy enough to sniff glue or

correction fluid—"the little kid drugs"—but that sometimes he and his friends would march up and down the aisles of supermarkets inhaling from spray cans. "Whipped cream was my favorite."

"Cocaine was great; I loved it," Mark reported. "But, I don't know, my dad had a role here. He was really against cocaine. He was against all drugs, but they were having a lot of problems with coked-up employees in his company, and he talked about cocaine a lot. So I never used it much. It was like using it meant I was going past a certain boundary of his that I didn't want to pass, if you know what I mean."

Kimberly, unfortunately, never had such boundaries. She has used all drugs at one time or another, and mostly smokes crack, but she also injects cocaine, or a combination of heroin and cocaine. "Yeah, one of these days it will get me," she conceded. "So, you think I care?"

"Yes, I do think you care," I answered.

"Well, you're wrong."

"So why are you here?"

"To check you out, give you the latest on what's goin' on out there. Maybe 'cause I want to care. Maybe I think you'll be able to make me care."

"I'd give my right arm to be able to do that. Will you come back more often?"

"Probably not."

That was a couple of months ago, and I haven't heard from Kimberly since. Kimberly wants out of her addiction. That's why she keeps coming back. But alone she cannot see her way out and I alone cannot help her. Our brief, sporadic encounters are no match for the power of the chemicals.

Even though Kimberly has gone the whole distance with drugs, she resembles every other young person harmfully involved with chemicals in that she wants out. *They all want out.* Although their defenses and their denial usually conceal—both from themselves and others—the deep pain they experience, their pain eventually seeps through. I've seen, time and time again, these kids tune into their pain, lower their guard, and admit that they need help, that they want out, but that they don't know how to get out.

Usually, however, all we see is the child's defensive structure, his bravado insistence that chemicals are not a problem, that everyone else is all messed up. Once adults recognize the child's chemical involvement, they can learn the steps needed to get behind the defensive structure to the hidden pain, so they can motivate their unmotivated child to agree to accept treatment.

Behavior/Personality Changes Associated with Adolescent Chemical Dependency

Addiction is the great equalizer. It causes very different adolescents to become alike, so alike that a behavior/personality profile can be drawn. As adolescents enter into addiction, their chemical use will remain covert or largely invisible. Yet at the same time, the behavior and personality changes caused by their harmful chemical involvement will be visible to any observer. Their behavior will become predictable.

Since it is easy to see the behavior and personality changes but not the chemical use, parents become puzzled, then agitated. Even though they take all kinds of actions in an attempt to get their child back to his former self, they fail. *Addressing the visible changes while ignoring the invisible causes is futile.*

If you have a child about whom you are concerned, note the behavior/personality changes your child is making and compare those changes with the behavior/personality profile associated with adolescent chemical dependency, which includes these six hallmarks: *isolation from family, association with known users or "troubled" peers, increased anger, nonengagement, nonmodification*, and *depression*.

The chemically dependent adolescent in our profile typically will become *isolated from his family*; he'll spend most of his time alone in his room and will want to avoid family meals, activities, and extended-family visits. He will leave—or be abandoned by—former friends and will start to *associate with known users or "troubled" peers*, who are often older and whom he will not want exposed to his family. He will experience an *increased level of hostility*: he will be disrespectful of or defiant to parents, teachers, and rules; he will use profanity; he may become sullen, surly, verbally abusive, or physically violent. He will become *nonengaged*, so walled off from his own feelings that he will no longer share his life—ideas, interests, feelings, activities—with his family. In particular, he will avoid give-and-take dialogues about his behavior. He will become *nonmodifiable*; that is, he will make and break promises, and will shape up, but not stay shaped up. He will become *depressed*, speaking of or attempting suicide, and probably will demonstrate a marked loss of self-esteem.

Now let's consider the children we have met so far in the light of these six hallmarks.

Toni had certainly become increasingly angry at her mother, but she did not show isolation from her family, association with known users or "troubled" peers, or depression. And since she agreed she needed to get help and consistently modified her behavior, she does not show nonengagement or nonmodification. Toni does not fit the profile. Nor does Brian, who showed none of the hallmarks.

It's hard to forget about Ricky's chemical use, since it killed him. But long before his death, long before he quit school, he withdrew from his family, became markedly hostile, hung around with known users, did not stay shaped up, and was depressed. He fits the profile perfectly.

So does Allison. She isolated herself from her family, associated with older "troubled" peers, became increasingly hostile, refused to be engaged, made and broke promises continuously, and looked depressed.

It's strange how one set of parents will ignore a child's grossly deviant behavior while another will take action quickly. Ignoring, by the way, includes overlooking the simple fact that home remedies are not working. I knew Ricky's parents well. I know they felt as much love for Ricky as Allison's parents felt for her. But, except for a brief time, they were not prepared to go beyond ineffective home remedies.

Some parents simply are not prepared to take more drastic action. They are sure they have, or soon will have, a way that works, despite failure after failure. Many of these parents are adult children of alcoholics or other dysfunctional parents. They often report feeling as powerless in the face of their child's addiction as they felt in the face of their own parent's addiction—or other dysfunction.

Whatever the situation, feeling love for children who become harmfully involved with chemicals is *not enough*. Adolescents require *love that is put into action*—action specifically designed to meet the needs of their condition. Such action includes determining appropriate treatment (see Chapter 9), reclaiming parental authority and ceasing to enable chemical dependency (see Chapter 10), providing a controlled environment with clear rules and a contract, if necessary (see Chapter 11), and creating a structured intervention and getting an adolescent to an appropriate treatment facility (see Chapter 12).

Let's continue our examination of the adolescents we met previously in light of the profile. Brad showed all the hallmarks: he isolated, associated with known users, was hostile, allowed virtually no engagement, never consistently modified his behavior, and was depressed.

Brad's parents put their love into action—misguided action. To Barbara and John, it certainly seemed as if Brad suffered from ''impulse disorder,'' one of the many psychiatric labels he was given. They were relieved when Brad agreed to see a psychiatrist, who became virtually the only person they could turn to during Brad's many crises. It took a couple of years, and much more blatant evidence of chemical use, for Barbara and John to begin to suspect that Brad's chemical use was causing his ''craziness.'' They all would have been better served if Brad's chemical use had been investigated at the outset, before his psychiatric treatment was initiated.

It was much easier for Bill, Mark's father, to initiate a course of action since Mark's use of marijuana had become visible at school. Thus the headmaster's suggestion that Mark's chemical use be evaluated made perfect sense to Bill, especially since Mark had already been expelled from another school for the same reason. But even before that, Mark had begun to show most, if not all, of the hallmarks in the profile of chemical dependency. He was more isolated, did not share his life as readily with his father, evidenced increased anger, and made promises he did not keep. While he was not seriously depressed, he did sometimes appear sad and sullen. It was unclear whether he was gravitating toward a more heavily using crowd.

No one in Kimberly's family cared enough about her to even notice her changes. Her chemical use from the beginning was so blatant that an initial screening tool like the profile would have been superfluous.

You need to consider the profile as an initial screen, a somewhat sketchy outline of how kids behave when they become harmfully involved with chemicals. If you are concerned about your son or daughter, *write down the hallmarks you have observed*.

Then for a fuller picture with more brushstrokes, go over the checklist of Behavior/Personality Changes Associated with Addiction on page 84. As you examine this list you will notice that it concentrates on behavior and personality changes and does not include signs of actual or suspected chemical use. That's something we'll get to later.

As you study the list, *concentrate on the concept of change.* If your child has always been a poor student, for example, then disregard that issue and concentrate solely on the recent changes in his behavior.

Just because children become teenagers does not mean they change their basic personality structure. Yes, teenagers have mood swings in response to outer events. Yes, they tug at parents' apron strings, bickering endlessly over everything. But healthy teenagers *do not* become strangers to their own parents.

Adolescents who repeatedly manifest the changes on the checklist inevitably become unpredictable aliens in their own households. They go beyond the realm of what is standard in adolescence.

Now, let's examine the children we have met so far in the light of this list, noting the changes reported by their parents. We will exclude, at this point, changes directly associated with known or suspected chemical use, such as Toni's broken leg or Brian's stash of marijuana.

Toni ran away from home once.

Brian showed none of the changes on the list.

Ricky repeatedly cut school classes and school days, associated with known users, quit school and virtually stopped functioning, stole from his parents, was verbally and physically violent, lied, and made and broke promises not to use heroin.

Allison was tardy, got lower grades, and turned in incomplete assignments. She was defiant and disrespectful of teachers, parents, and rules and she joined a "troubled" peer group. She had abrupt, inexplicable mood swings and deteriorating hygiene (her room was a mess), used profanity, and made and broke promises regarding personal change.

Brad broke curfews, stayed out without permission or notification, had abrupt, inexplicable mood swings, and committed a crime (arson). He turned in incomplete schoolwork; was suspended from school, was defiant and disrespectful of parents, teachers, and rules, and got lower grades. He wore the same clothes—showing signs of deteriorating hygiene—was physically and verbally violent, and stole from his parents.

Mark was suspended and expelled from school, slept for long periods during the day, had lower grades, gave up an extracurricular activity (jogging), made and broke promises not to drink, and was vague about the company he kept and his activities.

Since nothing much surfaced with Toni and Brian in light of the checklist, both are continuing to look healthy. In addition to exhibiting the hallmarks of the profile, Ricky, Allison, Brad, and Mark repeatedly show from six to seventeen characteristics on the list of behavior/personality changes, many of which are seriously deviant. At the very least, Ricky, Allison, Brad, and Mark no longer meet the criteria for good health. And since the changes in them are ones associated with adolescent addiction, it is safe for us to suspect that Ricky, Allison, Brad, and Mark are addicted. Although we have put our knowledge of their chemical use aside for the time being, we are able to still suspect addiction simply by observing their specific behavior/personality changes.

At this point you should have evaluated your child in terms of both the hallmarks of the adolescent addiction profile and the behavior/personality changes list. Is the picture any clearer? If your child is repeatedly showing several of the changes, at the very least he no longer meets the criteria for good health.

Again, put aside what you know about your child's chemical use and recall what you now know about healthy adolescents: *they do not repeatedly manifest the deviant or delinquent behavior as shown in the checklist.* Adolescents who look troubled *are* troubled. Do not, I implore you, ignore the changes you are seeing. Do not make Ramona's and Jim's mistake. Your child's life could depend on getting treatment. Pay attention to the changes you are seeing and do not depend on home remedies for the cure. Instead, *suspect chemical dependency*.

Do not attempt yet to seek treatment for your child. First, find out more about your child's chemical use. Chapter 7, "Signs of Alcohol and Other Drug Use," will show you how to actually detect chemical use by your teenager.

In the meantime, *do consider getting help for yourself*. Families Anonymous and Al-Anon are self-help groups for families of alcohol and drug-involved persons. Or attend meetings of Toughlove, a self-help group for parents of troubled adolescents, an estimated 90 percent of whom are addicted. All of these groups are listed in your telephone directory.

You do not need to be alone—and you should not be. Attempting to deal with this problem all by yourself will only weaken you. Addressing it with others will strengthen you and aid you in helping your child.

Everyone in these self-help groups I've mentioned has faced, or is facing, the same kinds of problems you are. They are there to help each other, and you. They will give you care, support, friendship, inspiration, guidance, and hope—and ask nothing in return. You won't even have to tell them your last name. If you wish, you may contribute toward expenses; otherwise, there is no cost involved. Usually, there is a speaker and a discussion at every meeting. You may ask questions or make comments, or just listen. At every meeting there are people who do all three.

You will be fearful as you contemplate entering a strange room (usually in a church, temple, or community center) full of strange people, but *do not let your fear paralyze you*. Everyone is afraid of attending a self-help group meeting for the first time. That's normal. Being dominated by the fear is not normal. So go!

BEHAVIOR/PERSONALITY CHANGES ASSOCIATED WITH ADDICTION

LAW (Charged or guilty of):

____ DWI (Driving While Intoxicated)

____ Shoplifting

____ MIP (Minor In Possession)

____ Vandalism

____ Dealing

____ Stealing

____ Assault and Battery

____ Prostitution

SCHOOL:

____ Drops or is suspended from extracurricular activities

____ Evidences increased tardiness

____ Cuts classes

____ Skips entire school day(s)

____ Turns assignments in late, incomplete, or not at all

____ Lets grades slip

____ Fails subjects

____ Forges passes or excuses

_____ Frequently leaves class
_____ Is inattentive or disruptive in class
_____ Sleeps in class
_____ Is defiant or disrespectful of teachers and rules
_____ Is suspended or expelled from school

SOCIAL:

_____ Uses "party" or "druggie" slang/lingo, such as
  • angel dust (a disassociative drug, also known as PCP)
  • wasted, stoned, or baked (a "high" state)
  • dope, ganga, herb, weed, reefer, pot, or grass (marijuana)
  • smack (heroin)
  • snow, line, rail, or coke (cocaine)
  • busted (being caught using or possessing drugs)
  • roach clips (devices for holding marijuana cigarette butts, or joints)
  • hash (a highly concentrated form of marijuana)
  • freebasing (refining cocaine into smokable form)
  • speed or uppers (amphetamines)
  • druggie (a regular user of drugs)
  • stash (a hidden supply of drugs)
  • toke (a single inhalation of marijuana)
  • trip (take a hallucinogenic drug, like LSD, mescaline, or peyote [mushroom])
  • downers (sedatives or tranquilizers)
_____ Abandons (or is left by) former friends
_____ Joins new "troubled" peers, or peers known to be users, who are often older
_____ Keeps new friends away from parents
_____ Has peers who hang up on parents or refuse to give names

FAMILY:

_____ Precipitates family fights/estrangement

_____ Stays out beyond curfews without permission/notification

_____ Stops doing assigned chores

_____ Sneaks out of house

_____ Stays out overnight (or for days) without permission/notification

_____ Refuses to obey family rules

_____ No longer shares activities with parents/becomes more secretive

_____ Withdraws from extended-family functions/visits

_____ Does not want to share meals with family

_____ Isolates; stays in room away from others

_____ Is vague about company kept and time spent

_____ Does not inform parents of school activities (open houses, teacher appointments, warnings, or suspensions)

_____ Has money; source unexplained

_____ Manipulates parents; plays one off against the other

_____ Is easily angered; parents "watch their words," "handle with kid gloves," or "walk on eggs"

_____ Uses profanity increasingly

_____ Becomes verbally abusive

_____ Becomes physically violent

_____ Shows increased level of hostility

_____ Is surly, sullen, refuses to speak

_____ Makes and breaks promises

_____ Is defiant or disrespectful of parents and rules

_____ Shapes up but does not stay shaped up

MENTAL:

____ Shows reduced attention span; problems with concentration

____ Is paranoid: believes being watched, under suspicion, or others out to get him/her

____ Has undefinable fears

____ Is agitated; has trouble sitting still

PHYSICAL:

____ Evidences weight changes; drastic loss or gain

____ Displays erratic sleeping habits; too much or too little

____ Stays up at night; sleeps during day

____ Has more frequent injuries/bruises

____ Displays deteriorating hygiene with regard to self or room

____ Wears same clothes from one day to the next

____ Has deep, nagging cough; dry persistent cough

____ Has increased respiratory ailments

____ Displays erratic or extreme eating habits

____ Shows reduced energy level

EMOTIONAL:

____ Speaks of death or suicide

____ Is increasingly moody; easily slighted

____ Sometimes is inexplicably happy or sad

____ Displays sudden and abrupt mood shifts

____ Does not share feelings; is defensive or "walled off"

_____ Becomes unreasonable; parents cannot get their points across; refuses to enter give-and-take dialogues about own behavior

_____ Seems sad, down, depressed

_____ Evidences increasing depression

_____ Speaks of self as "no good," "failure"

_____ Displays increasing level of hostility

_____ Loses interest in formerly valued activities

_____ Loses drive/motivation to succeed

_____ Shows reduced self-esteem; feels inadequate, not up to former performance level

_____ Is less hopeful; more cynical about life

ETHICAL:

_____ Present behavior in conflict with former values

_____ Lies, cheats

_____ Hocks own and/or others' possessions

_____ Steals from parents/siblings

_____ Displays blatant sexual behavior

_____ Has unplanned pregnancy; father may be unknown

_____ Loses interest in attending church; no longer will discuss own religious beliefs; no longer believes in God

SEVEN

Signs of Alcohol and Other Drug Use

If your child fits the profile and is repeatedly showing several of the related behavior/personality changes associated with adolescent addiction, it can't be easy for you. Not only are these kinds of changes worrisome, but they are exceedingly unpleasant to live with.

No doubt you have suffered one crisis after another in your household. You may see very clearly the danger your child is in, and you may be eager to get to the bottom of all of this.

But you may feel overwhelmed, full of shame and embarrassment. You may believe you have failed as a parent. Feeling discouraged, perhaps hopeless, you may be reluctant to look further.

Almost certainly you and the other members of your family are walking lightly around the child about whom you are so concerned. Kids in the process of these kinds of changes are scary, even intimidating. You, or others in your family, may crave peace. All of you may feel wary about investigating your child's chemical use. You may fear rocking the boat. You may want to put blinders on, and not look further.

But you must.

Once a teenager starts repeatedly showing the behavior/personality changes that indicate chemical dependency, a momentum develops. The more changes your child makes, the more changes are ahead, leading to a downward spiral. *Ignoring the changes will not make them go away; it will only allow more to develop*. If the changes exist, they exist. Accept that.

Is your child using alcohol and/or other drugs? How extensively? These are the questions you now have to answer, for only then can you bring a halt to your child's destructive momentum and introduce a new direction toward health.

You are now in the dark tunnel. Investigate your child's chemical use and you will come to the light at the end of the tunnel. There is a light, and that light is treatment and recovery. *But first comes detection and recognition.*

With this in mind, review the checklist of Known and Suspected Signs of Alcohol and Other Drug Use at the end of this chapter. Did you check any symptoms? If not, that does not mean chemical use does not exist; it only means you haven't uncovered it yet. Remember that *chemical use is covert*; it's largely invisible. This also means that if you've found some signs, more signs probably exist. If you uncover any evidence of chemical use at the beginning of your investigation, you've probably found only the tip of the iceberg.

In any case, *you need to probe further*. Ask your spouse to review the list of Signs of Known and Suspected Alcohol and Other Drug Use. It will not be at all unusual for one of you to know things the other doesn't. Ask your children to review the list. Tell them that you are trying to help, not hurt, the child about whom you are concerned. Promise that you won't reveal them as your source of information. Then, if you feel you need more proof, by all means look for more signs.

While I normally do not encourage parents to snoop, you have to do just that when investigating your child's chemical use. Ask yourself how actively you've looked for signs of chemical use in the past. Have you waited up for your child at night, or awakened to greet your child upon his return? If not, how can you know if he has been drinking? Start waiting up—take a good look, smell your teenager's breath, watch the way he walks and talks. Don't drink yourself, for you won't be able to smell alcohol on your child's breath.

What does your child do holed up in his room for hours on end? Go up, knock, enter, and sit down for a chat—regularly. Smell anything? (Marijuana? Alcohol? Incense?) Hear anything? (Slurring of words? Endless repetition, as if intoxicated?) See anything? (Cellophane packets? The remains of marijuana cigarettes in an ashtray? An open beer can? Pipes or razor blades?) What are the pupils of the eyes like? Dilated (from cocaine)? Constricted to pinpoints (from heroin)? Any problem focusing, as if drunk? An open window, in the middle of winter? What? Your child won't let you in? *Then it's almost certain there's a reason you should know about.*

How do you feel about searching your child's room? I hate the idea. When I was a child, my room was mine, my mail was mine, my diary was mine, and that felt good. It made me feel that my parents respected me. So I don't take such room searches lightly. In fact, I see them as an invasion, a psychic invasion of the worst sort. Nevertheless, I sometimes suggest a room search.

I never once searched the rooms of my three children. I don't even know if they had diaries. And I never read their mail. But if things had been urgent, if things had happened which led me to think their lives were threatened, I would have torn their rooms apart. I would have gone to any lengths to become informed.

Phyllis searched Allison's room after she discovered that some of their liquor supply was missing. I'm not sure I would have done that. I like to think that the missing liquor supply alone would have been enough to put me on the alert. Nevertheless, in retrospect, Phyllis is glad she investigated; finding that empty bottle of vodka shocked her to the core. More than anything, it made her realize that Allison's drinking was a very serious matter.

When Phyllis and her husband brought Allison to me, they told me they were aware of these signs: alcohol on breath; missing parental alcohol supply; vodka bottle hidden in her room; stumbling/staggering gait; breath deodorizers (gum); and reports of drinking from camp counselors and a friend's mother. Six signs altogether, some of which were repeatedly observed. Now watch the iceberg of chemical use emerge during our first session.

Petite, pretty, dark-haired, dark-eyed, wearing very little or no makeup, Allison looked like she should be in front of the class reciting poetry, not raiding the liquor cabinet. Although she denied feeling scared, she did say that she couldn't see why she was meeting with me. She thought her parents were making a big fuss over nothing. I told her that I wanted to trace her alcohol and drug consumption from the time of first use. Allison said she didn't use drugs. I also promised her that I would not reveal specifics of her chemical use, but that at the end of our session, I would want to give her parents my opinion about what I thought her use meant—the summation without the details. Allison agreed to talk about her alcohol use under this condition but explained, "It's my mom. She exaggerates everything."

According to Allison, she had her first beer in fifth grade, when she was ten. Some boys had brought beer into the backyard of a friend who was having a party. "We snuck out of the house, drank the beer, went back into the party . . . in and out." Allison had watched kids drink at other parties when the adults were not around. "It looked like fun and I wanted to see what it was like. It was nice. I liked it a lot." She admitted that since then she has looked for the opportunity to drink at parties. She said she helped raise money for purchasing beer and reluctantly admitted that she occasionally stole from her mother's purse or used her lunch money to buy alcohol. She also said that if she and her friends could not get an older kid to buy the beer for them, or if they could not raise enough money, they would look for, and usually find, ways to raid parental alcohol supplies at various parties.

Allison said that she "occasionally" drank alcohol after school at friends' homes starting in the seventh grade. When asked what "occasionally" meant, she said, "Once a month or so." With further questioning, she admitted, "Maybe once a week in the eighth grade." She denied drinking alcohol daily at friends' homes but admitted she sometimes raided her parents' liquor cabinet after school or at night when they were asleep—"once a week or so." Allison said that when she drank, she usually drank a lot, especially at parties. "Everyone does. That's what you do: drink everything that's there."

Allison said that alcohol occasionally interfered with her functioning. Sometimes she felt sick the next day at school and was not overly interested in what the teachers were saying. Although she thought alcohol helped her study at home, she then admitted that she often fell asleep before completing her assignments.

Allison looked sad when she admitted that her former friends didn't like her anymore. "But who cares? They're not worth bothering about." She admitted that they had complained to her about her drinking. She also said that she didn't like the older kids she was now hanging around with all that much, but "at least they're friendly to me." And she agreed these new friends like to drink beer. "But some of them drink too much . . . all day long in school. I hope you don't think I drink like that."

Allison had, in fact, progressed to a pattern of regular heavy use (five or more drinks at a time one or more times a week), a pattern that seemed on the increase. When viewed collectively—beer or other forms of alcohol at parties on Friday and Saturday nights, at friends' homes after school "maybe once a week," and at her own home "once a week or so"— Allison's drinking represented a rather massive iceberg.

Like Allison, adolescents in an evaluation will usually reveal much more of their chemical use than they intend. Occasionally, like Mark, they talk eagerly. Before Bill brought Mark in for an evaluation, he had observed six signs altogether: alcohol odor on breath (repeatedly); alcohol intoxication (repeatedly); passed out (once); chronic red eyes; erratic sleep habits (several hours after school, which could indicate chronic marijuana lethargy); and several reports of marijuana use from schools. Any one of these signs, coupled with Mark's behavior/personality changes, is serious enough to warrant professional evaluation.

But now look at what we learned about Mark's chemical use during his evaluation: hard liquor every weekend; two to three beers every day; daily marijuana use, virtually around the clock; blackouts; and admission of being unable to stop. Although many parents might not have considered Mark's six signs as significant indicators of chemical use, most would be appalled at Mark's actual intake, or his hidden chemical use. I can't emphasize enough how crucial it is to keep the concept of icebergs constantly in mind when examining adolescent chemical use. *So much more will be hidden than is apparent.*

Mark was unusual in his willingness to talk freely about his chemical use. Often adolescents are stubborn and defensive, and even upon professional evaluation their icebergs do not immediately surface.

Look at the case of David, a seventeen-year-old prep school junior when I first met him. A few days prior to our appointment, his mother had taken him to the doctor because David was having "a strange kind of anxiety attack." He was having trouble breathing, was extremely agitated, and the arteries in his neck were visibly throbbing. The doctor, testing him for drugs, found traces of cocaine and referred David and his mother to me for further evaluation.

David's mother, Karen, knew that he occasionally drank beer on weekends, but she had no information relating to any additional chemical use. She was concerned about his arrogant attitude, which seemed to be a relatively new development, but otherwise thought David was on the right track. He was doing well in school as far as she knew, was involved with a "good bunch" of friends, had many interests, including their community's drama club, and was not in any way a problem child.

David was cool—arrogant, just like his mother had said. Throughout our interview he seemed above it all, even amused. He claimed that he had used cocaine only once—when he had the anxiety attack. "I wanted to see if coke was the big deal everyone said it was." He said he sometimes drank beer after rehearsals on weekends, but as often as not drank soda. "Getting drunk is not my idea of fun." He reported that he first started drinking beer in the eighth grade and acknowledged using other forms of alcohol on occasion. "Who doesn't?" David qualified this response by saying that he drank wine with his family at holiday dinners, champagne at weddings, and hard liquor occasionally with friends, adding that he preferred beer. He said that he tried marijuana "a couple of times" during his freshman years in high school but did not particularly like it, and claimed he had not used it since. He denied ever using any other kind of chemical.

David was so glib, so well defended, that I could not help wondering what he was hiding. Kids who try cocaine are usually far more heavily involved with alcohol or marijuana than

David admitted to. But he was like the Rock of Gibraltar; I couldn't get anything more out of him.

I reviewed both lists—Signs of Known and Suspected Alcohol and Other Drug Use (see page 101) and the Behavior/Personality Changes Associated with Addiction (see page 84)—with Karen so that she could evaluate the present situation and know what to look for in the future. She did not note any other signs of chemical use, but she did report that David stayed in his room a lot, preferred eating alone, was sometimes sullen, and occasionally would refuse to speak to her. However, she didn't consider this behavior significant. "This is the way he's always been—at least since he's been a teenager," she said. "I don't think he's changed." At the end of the session, David promised not to use alcohol or other drugs in the future. His mother agreed to bring him back if he broke his promise.

Three months later, mother and son were back. In the interim, Karen had found a packet of rolling papers underneath his dresser. Then she found three empty beer cans outside the window of his room, which hadn't been there the week before when she'd weeded the flower beds. When she finally found a cellophane packet coated with white powder on the seat of her car which David had borrowed the previous evening, she brought him back to see me.

At least in Karen's eyes, David didn't match the profile typical of adolescent addiction. She believed that the items she checked on the behavior/personality list were not significant because they were part of his usual teenage demeanor. She was not willing to think that David might have started using chemicals prior to becoming a teenager, and prior to the changes. Her only concern was his increased arrogance, a change that's not even on the list. But now she was also concerned about the increased signs of chemical use.

During my first interview with David I'd noticed that he was not engageable in any manner whatsoever. Walled off from his feelings, he reported his many accomplishments but denied problems of any kind and only admitted to drinking beer "on occasion."

During my second interview David was exceedingly hostile. He said that he'd broken his promises because "they were stupid to begin with," and indicated he had no intentions of making similar promises in the future. He maintained that the white powder was not cocaine, and said that I was stupid to think the cellophane packet could be considered drug paraphernalia. Besides, it wasn't his. "How the hell do I know where it came from? It could be hers, you know," he retorted, pointing to his mother. He also said that he had nothing to do with the beer cans or the rolling papers. "The only thing you've got is circumstantial evidence. You think you can convict me on that?"

Before taking further action, Karen wanted to consult David's father, Cliff, from whom she was divorced. Fortunately, Cliff took the "circumstantial evidence" seriously. He spoke to the headmaster and the teachers at David's school, many of whom were beginning to have concerns. While David was still doing good schoolwork, they mentioned the number of classes he was cutting, and wondered why his mother was so readily excusing him. As it turned out, it was David who was writing the excuses. Several teachers spoke of his arrogance and surliness, one finding David newly defiant toward her assignment rules. "If he doesn't approve, he simply ignores them. He wasn't like this at the beginning of the year." The headmaster reported that David's best friend had been caught snorting cocaine in class and had been expelled the week before.

David's iceberg emerged ever so slowly, and only because

his parents went to great lengths to carefully investigate his chemical use.

In contrast, JoAnn's iceberg was readily apparent—at least to her mother and older brother, if not her father.

Several times over the past three years, JoAnn, nineteen, arrived home drunk on weekend nights. Once several hulking, football-player types carried her home in the middle of the night. She was so drunk that she was nearly comatose. Greg, her older brother, had been concerned about her drinking for years. He told his parents that JoAnn always drank more than anyone else at parties, and that she was always the first to suggest getting high. He also reported that several of his friends had seen JoAnn snorting cocaine on many different occasions over the past year when she was home on college breaks. Moreover, Greg himself had occasionally seen JoAnn in bars with much older men, both during high school and this year, her first in college.

JoAnn's mother, Sue Ellen, insisted when I first met her that JoAnn had a problem with alcohol and maybe with cocaine. She wanted something done about it. "I don't like seeing my daughter like this. I question her values. We're a churchgoing family and . . . well . . . she's become loose, like she's a harlot. JoAnn actually brags about her sexual exploits and ridicules me for being prissy. I'm ashamed of her, but I'm also scared, scared to death. She could get AIDS, for crying out loud. But she just laughs and doesn't seem to care. She doesn't seem to care about anything anymore. She was a champion swimmer in high school, and now she's dropped off the swim team. I don't even know who her friends are. When she's home from college and goes out, more often than not she's drunk when she comes in."

JoAnn's father, Matt, believed that his wife and son were exaggerating. "It's a new age out there," he said. "JoAnn's not doing anything her friends aren't doing." When I reviewed the data his wife reported, he scoffed, "That goes with being nineteen. Leave her alone; she'll settle down."

JoAnn, whom I saw separately on that same visit, thought the whole thing was a joke. She denied using cocaine, admitted to drinking "like everyone else," and insisted she could quit any time she wished. She had a multitude of explanations for her changing behavior, none of which had anything to do with chemical use, and accused her mother and Greg of exaggerating. "You should listen to my dad. Mom's crazy, and so's Greg."

Despite their conflicting claims, JoAnn's parents agreed to bring her back for an alcohol and other drug history, a basic part of any chemical dependency evaluation. Shortly thereafter, JoAnn disappeared.

Sue Ellen called to report that JoAnn had taken off for three days, without permission or notification. "We have no idea where she's been. She came home early this morning but says it's none of our business. She looks terrible. She's filthy . . . and so are her clothes. She was so listless and weak when she came in she could barely make it to her room. And then she just fell into bed. She didn't even take off her filthy clothes, and she didn't shower."

It was obvious to both of us that something serious was going on. I suspected that JoAnn had probably been on a crack binge and that now she was crashing, but I was fairly certain that Matt would want to overlook this, just as he had everything else. That morning, when Sue Ellen called to report that JoAnn was home, he said, "Let it go. Get off her back." I told Sue Ellen that I thought they had an urgent problem on their hands and a room search was warranted. She agreed. Matt reluctantly agreed once I told him of my suspicion of crack use. I asked Sue Ellen to search the room at the first opportunity and to confiscate anything at all that might point to chemical use, including JoAnn's diary and any letters that might be lying around. She and Matt were then to come to see me.

Sue Ellen didn't find anything except JoAnn's high school diary, which told a sordid story: alcohol use since seventh grade; stealing money from parents, siblings, and friends; cocaine snorting since eleventh grade; almost daily cocaine snorting during her senior year; dealing cocaine; prostitution; two abortions; and repeated thoughts of suicide.

Sue Ellen had read the diary before our appointment. Matt had refused. Once I read it to him, he seemed to deflate right before my eyes, like a punctured balloon. They both wept, and they agreed to work together to help JoAnn.

Searching a child's room is a serious invasion of privacy. *Nevertheless, a room search can save a child's life*. If things are desperate, and you have not found sufficient evidence of chemical use thus far, by all means search your child's room.

You might also choose to do as David's father did. Go to your child's school and tell them of your concerns about your child's behavior and personality changes. Tell them you need help. Ask them what they've noticed about your child. Show them both of the checklists in this book. Promise them that you will not reveal individual sources of information.

Once you have collected all possible data, your next step is to connect the chemical use to the behavior/personality changes. Then you should get professional assistance to assess the extent of the involvement and determine the most appropriate treatment. And since most children harmfully involved with chemicals are uncooperative, you will most likely need help getting your child to do what needs to be done.

Seek out an addiction specialist, someone educated and trained in chemical dependency, who has experience in adolescent chemical dependency assessment, intervention, and treatment. You can call the local affiliate of the National Council on Alcoholism (see Appendix B) for names of addiction specialists. Or call hospitals in your area that have chemical dependency treatment units, or freestanding chemical dependency treatment centers, or out-patient alcohol and other drug facilities. These organizations will be listed in your phone directory and will be able to lead you to an addiction specialist, in their own facility, in an outside agency, or in private practice.

SIGNS OF KNOWN AND SUSPECTED ALCOHOL AND OTHER DRUG USE

SIGNS OF KNOWN ALCOHOL AND OTHER DRUG USE:

____ Alcohol on breath

____ Blackouts; functions but does not remember

____ Slurred words

____ Stumbling, staggering gait

____ Unfocused eyes

____ Rambling or repetitive talk

____ Vomitus with alcohol odor

____ Track marks (heroin)

____ Dilated pupils (cocaine)

____ Constricted pupils (heroin)

____ Reports from others of observed chemical use

____ Snorting, smoking, swallowing, or injecting a chemical

____ Overdose (comatose state following use)

SIGNS OF SUSPECTED ALCOHOL AND OTHER DRUG USE:

____ Nodding out

____ Remnants of white powder on upper lip (cocaine)

____ Chronically red eyes (marijuana)

____ Sweet, cloying marijuana odor on clothes or in room

____ Passing out

____ Shakes/tremors

_____ Nasal congestion; nosebleeds

_____ Wired, taut, strung out (cocaine)

_____ Brown-stained fingers (marijuana)

_____ Bizarre paranoid suspicions (cocaine psychosis)

_____ State of extreme panic

_____ Jerkiness, twitching, can't sit still

_____ Chronic lethargy (marijuana)

_____ Unusual weight gain or loss

_____ Seizures

_____ Missing or watered-down parental alcohol supply

_____ Missing parental tranquilizer, sedative, narcotic supply

_____ Small cellophane packets with a white powdery dust (cocaine)

_____ Slightly larger cellophane packets with remnants of oregano-like leaves, stems, seeds

_____ Beer cans, wine and liquor bottles in room

_____ Straight-edged razor blade (for lining up cocaine "hit")

_____ Tiny spoon, often worn around neck (for snorting cocaine)

_____ Small glass or plastic vial with brightly colored screw-on top (crack)

_____ Double bowl pipe (bottom for water, top for crack)

_____ Small porcelain pipes (marijuana)

_____ Bongs (tall, often brightly colored, plastic or brass water pipes for marijuana or hashish)

_____ Cigarette rolling papers (for making marijuana roaches)

_____ Roach clip (for holding marijuana cigarette)

_____ Incense (to cover marijuana odor)

_____ Visine or other eye drops (marijuana)

_____ Breath deodorizers/gum (alcohol)

_____ Pills of various shapes, sizes, and colors

_____ Pea-sized chunks of whitish-gray soaplike substance
(crack)
_____ Syringe (for injecting cocaine, heroin, or both)

Connecting Chemical Use to Behavior/Personality Changes

Parents need to know two important facts about adolescents who repeatedly show some signs of chemical use and several behavior/personality changes.

Fact number one: *There is a cause and effect relationship between chemical use and behavior/personality changes.*

Fact number two: *The adolescent needs treatment.*

Although these two facts may seem obvious, unfortunately they are not readily apparent to many of the parents I've known. Some parents have a lot of trouble putting the two halves of fact number one together; they just cannot seem to see the cause and effect relationship at all. And while they want their child to shape up, they usually do not see that their child needs treatment.

The majority do manage to see the cause and effect relationship, but nonetheless they are confused. They do not know which is cause and which is effect, which is primary and which is secondary. Consequently, while it is usually clear to them that their child needs help, they often seek the wrong kind of treatment.

Finally, there are those parents who are quite clear about both of the above facts. Almost certain that the changes result from their child's chemical use, they know their child needs help specifically for addiction. But most do not know how to get their child to agree to seek treatment.

All parents of those adolescents who repeatedly show several signs of chemical use and behavior/personality changes are at a critical juncture. The path they choose to follow can either facilitate or impede their child's recovery.

Let's talk about parents who see signs of chemical use and behavior and personality changes, but who fail to put the two together. They do not see the connection—at least in any way that makes sense. Their reasoning is often circuitous, or hard to follow. When I meet with such parents, I must always bear in mind that what they want from me is usually not at all what they need.

Recently a bright, highly articulate mother came to see me. She reported several signs of her fifteen-year-old son's chemical use over the past year and a half. One of these was drug dealing. Her observations, as well as those of others, indicated that he was using alcohol, marijuana, cocaine, and other unidentified drugs. The mother also reported such persistent deviant behavior and personality changes that she and her husband, having lost all parental authority in their household, had gone to court in an attempt to get some control over their child.

Now under house arrest, the fifteen-year-old can leave the premises only to attend school. No more evenings out. No more trips to New York City's drug discos. No more contact with his girlfriend, no more verbal abuse, no more dealing, no more alcohol and other drug use, and no more contact with his "druggie" friends. If he violates any of these rules, his parents and the court can decide to send him to a court-appointed home for wayward boys, or a school for emotionally disturbed adolescents.

"Have you considered that your son might be addicted?" I asked.

"Absolutely not," she replied. "He's not using at all now."

"Right now he can't use . . . maybe. After all, you've got him under house arrest. But what about the past year and a half—did you ever suspect his behavior resulted from his chemical use?"

"No, not at all. He's a genius. His IQ is so high I don't want to embarrass you by telling you what it is, but . . ."

"I won't be embarrassed. You can tell me."

"His IQ is 148."

"That's great. But I'm not sure why you think being a genius provides him with immunity from addiction."

"You don't understand. He's gifted, absolutely gifted. He's so talented, so artistic. And he's also a scientist. I dare say he knows more about the molecular structure of drugs than you do. He's even made some of his own drugs." A spin to the girlfriend. "Everyone who knows her says the same thing, that she's an addicted slut. But don't think I normally talk about people this way; even Richard, our friend from the mayor's office, says the same thing." Then a spin to her son's friends, while I'm still wondering what drugs her kid has made. "They're a problem, of course, at least they were. Right now one's in a chemical dependency treatment center and the other one's in Israel. His parents sent him there because they thought he wouldn't be able to use drugs on a kibbutz, but his mother told me last week that my son has been sending him drugs. Can you imagine the nerve of these kids?" Off on another spin, back to his IQ. "He's bright. I told you he's only fifteen, but what you don't know is that by the end of next year, when he graduates from high school, he'll also receive his associate's degree from college."

"So?" I asked, feeling dizzy.

"Oh, this is so frustrating," she answered. "You're just like the others. You don't understand what being a genius means, do you?"

"Does it mean he can't become addicted?"

"Well, you have to know him. He's . . ."

"Why are you here?" I interrupted. "What do you want from me?"

"I want you to tell me when we can trust him again. We want to start easing up on the house arrest. That's why I brought him with me today, so you could meet him, talk to him . . ."

Interrupting her once again, I was direct. "You're a very powerful woman. You're attempting to force me to do what you want—but I don't believe what you want is what you need.

"First, I can't answer your question. House arrest is not treatment. It doesn't turn an untrustworthy child into a trustworthy child. About all it does is keep the top on the volcano. It might buy you time to find out what your child needs, but it's not going to do anything more than that. So, if determining your child's trustworthiness is the issue, I can't help you. Second, *you're not asking the right question*. Third, I told you on the phone not to bring your son along with you today. Why did you bring him?"

"Because I thought if you saw him—just spoke to him— you'd see how unique he is, and then you'd be able to help. And he might listen to you; you've written books and he might respect that."

"Well, books aren't magic wands. Only *you* can get his attention, and you're not going to be able to do that if you continue on the same track. I don't doubt that your child is unique. And I did see him briefly as he headed off into the waiting room. His eyes are rheumy, or red. If he doesn't have a cold or an allergy of some kind, you'd be wise to suspect that he's still using marijuana, despite your house arrest. Also, he's dressed like a punk. His lips turned up into a snarl when I introduced myself, and he refused to shake hands with me.

None of this means he's addicted, but he sure looks and acts as if he might be. The question you should be asking—'Is my son addicted?'—isn't even on your agenda. You've talked in circles here today, but at home you seemed to have concentrated on controlling your son's behavior. Are you interested in seeing if his chemical use is the cause of that behavior?''

"No, that misses the point," she answered. "You're the third person I've seen. Your name kept cropping up and I thought you'd be the one who'd understand my son. But you're just like the others.''

"Are you scared? I know I would be if I were in your shoes. Is it frightening to think your child might be addicted?''

"No, it's not frightening; it just overlooks the nature of my son's mind. He's different. He's not like other kids.''

"But you have him under house arrest. *Juvenile delinquents get put under house arrest, not geniuses*. Is the question too simple? Is it perhaps too simple for you to think that your son's behavior might be the result of his chemical use?''

"Perhaps," she admitted.

"Are you disappointed with me?''

"Yes.''

"Are you willing to address this simple question anyway?''

"I don't seem to have much choice," she answered in a resigned tone. "I had such high hopes when I heard about you, and now you're telling me what everyone else has told me.''

I won't even attempt to analyze the circuitous thinking that has kept this mother from putting cause and effect together in any way that makes sense. Fortunately, she seems ready to begin seeing that her son's behavior might be the result of his chemical use. Besides, she beginning to see that house arrest is not the panacea she hoped for. She knows it cannot go on forever and she's afraid—justifiably so—that her son will return to his former behavior once she lets up and she does not like to even think of the court-mandated options if that should happen.

Now let's look at the parents in our case studies to see how well they comprehended the two facts. JoAnn's father knew about her use of alcohol and cocaine and her many behavior/ personality changes, yet he minimized their significance and adamantly refused to entertain the idea of a connection between the drug abuse and personality changes. It was only when he was faced with her diary that he was willing to make the connection and see her need for a treatment that was specific to her harmful chemical involvement.

Ricky's parents knew for years—not months, not weeks, not days—that he was a heroin user. Ricky had become a virtual vegetable, a nonfunctioning, barely alive teenager, yet Ramona and Jim still were not able to see his condition clearly. They berated, begged, nagged, threatened, and slapped him around for using heroin. Ramona tried to make his life easier, while Jim tried to get him to be a man, to get a job and grow up. They seemed to place his heroin use in one compartment and his behavior in another, as if they were separate entities. Occasionally over the years they put the two together, yet they still didn't recognize Ricky's need for treatment.

Neither did Tim's parents.

Mary, Tim's mother, cried throughout our first session. She said that she could not bear to think about Tim's chemical problems, although she had been the one to insist that Tim had a problem and needed help. His father, Marty, who sat as far away from us as he could get, had little to contribute— neither tears nor comments. Occasionally he would correct Mary or throw in a tidbit about Tim's behavior, but mostly

he showed impatience—at both Mary's tears and Tim's behavior. A couple of times, Marty ridiculed Mary, and her
tears increased.

Both were in a lot of pain—handling it differently, but handling it as best they could. Then twenty-four, Tim should have
been at the peak of life. He wasn't. He would venture out of
his room to grab food from the refrigerator when no one was
around, but mostly he did little else other than use alcohol and
other drugs.

Tim originally had been the most ambitious of their four
children; he wanted to be a lawyer and, hopefully, one day a
U.S. senator. But Tim flunked out of college during his second
semester, and his life has been going downhill ever since.

Their oldest child, Gene, a recovering alcoholic, is thirty-
one, married, and the owner of a landscape design company.
He is living his life pretty much as he wishes, despite his former bout with alcoholism.

Peggy, twenty-seven, was married right after high school.
She now has three children and lives in another state. There's
not much about her life that she would change, but she is sad
about one thing from her past. When Tim was eleven, she and
one of her cousins gave him so much champagne at an uncle's
wedding that he got drunk. "I wish we hadn't done that,"
she says. "We thought it was funny at the time, but now I
feel guilty, like maybe we started Timmy off. After that, at
other family gatherings, I'd see Tim running around, sneak-
ing sips out of other people's drinks."

At twenty-two, Jenny is the youngest. She lives at home,
works full time as a hostess/cashier, and goes to the local community college part time. She'd change everything about her
life if she could. "I want to get away from there, out of that
crazy house. I'm sick of my brother and I'm sick of the way
my parents treat him. They don't do anything right. They let
Tim get away with everything."

According to Mary, Tim had always been a cheerful child, "a born optimist," and a good student. If not the brightest of their children, Tim was "certainly the quickest." But soon after entering high school, he lost his former cheerfulness, becoming uncommunicative and rebellious. He broke curfews repeatedly, often came home intoxicated, started swearing at his parents, and launched scathing verbal attacks on Jenny. Tim's interest in school fell, and so did his grades. He cut classes and was suspended several times. He spent a lot of time in the principal's office, on detention for one thing or another, but finally graduated with good enough grades to get into the state university.

Mary and Marty were, of course, aware that Tim drank alcohol in high school, but they were not concerned since they never saw any evidence of other drug use. Marty admits that not only did he consider alcohol to be safe, but he somehow assumed that if Tim was drinking, he wasn't doing drugs.

Jenny knew otherwise. "I could see the whole thing. By the time he was a senior, Tim was drinking or smoking pot all the time—before school, between classes, before football practice, after practice, on his way home, and then in his room every night. Jesus, there were pot fumes all over the house."

Jenny reports feeling shamed by her brother when they were in high school together. "He was known as a druggie. He was wasted and everyone knew it. Sometimes I'd cry; we'd always been so close and it was a very sad thing to watch. But I was scared to tell my parents because Tim always threatened to beat on me, and I knew he would, too. Anyway, it wouldn't have done any good. I passed a lot of hints, but they didn't want to hear me. Once when Tim was having one of his freak-outs and got in a fistfight with Dad, I told Mom to get smart . . . like, what did she think all the incense was for? She said something stupid, like it smelled nice. I told her it was to cover the pot odor, but obviously she didn't want to hear that."

Mary reported that Tim was full of plans to become a chef after he got kicked out of college. He had always liked cooking, and, despite his chemical use, had prepared many of the family meals when he was younger. Although he got a job as an assistant cook in a local restaurant, he was fired after several months. "I guess he wasn't showing up on time," Mary said. "Because he was stoned on pot," Marty added. And that's the way it went for Tim: short-lived jobs with an ever-increasing span of time between positions.

Everyone in Tim's family spoke to him at different times about his chemical use. They pleaded with him to get help, but he always adamantly refused. Gene took Tim to an Alcoholics Anonymous meeting on his twenty-first birthday, three years ago. He told Tim that AA was the greatest gift he could ever ask for, but Tim was not impressed. Finally, Gene advised the family to give up: "No one can help him until he wants help."

Mary said that she and Marty always assumed Tim would eventually do as Gene had done—join AA and get himself straightened out. Even when that didn't seem to be happening, they still looked upon Gene as a reliable authority on alcohol and other drug problems and continued to believe he was right when he said nothing could be done until Tim wanted help.

Marty once talked Tim into working for him in his dry-cleaning shop but had to let him go after a few weeks. "He wouldn't learn, not even the easiest things, like what goes where," Marty said. He left the tickets out of the clothing bags, mixed the clothes up, argued with the customers . . . and that's when he was in the store. Most of the time he was sitting out on the back stoop drinking beer and smoking pot. I told him if he smoked that stuff at my shop, I'd call the police, but he smoked it anyway. So I got rid of him."

One thing Marty did insist on was that Tim keep up the

lawn at home. As Mary said, "Tim was very good at that. Our neighbors used to tell us how good our property looked with all the pretty shrubs and flowers. They congratulated us on what a fine job we'd done raising Tim. I just couldn't tell them what was really going on . . . I guess I was too ashamed."

For the past year, about all that Tim has done is work on the lawn "a few hours a week." He has not looked for a job in several months. Marty has kept up his car and insurance payments because "he'll need a car when he gets a job." Marty also gives Tim an allowance for doing the lawn, and even though it's only a March-to-November job, he pays Tim year-round. "I took the total of what he'd earn for the nine months and divided it by twelve so he'd have an even pay schedule throughout the year."

Mary admitted that she frequently gave Tim "an extra dollar or two when he ran short." Jenny says he ran short almost every day and "it's more than a dollar or two. Jesus, he works on the lawn a few hours a week, tops, and he's getting more than I'm getting. And I work every damn day of the year, just about."

Jenny had already told her parents that Tim bought alcohol and drugs when he left the house every afternoon, but they each gave a variety of excuses for shelling out the cash. Marty said, "He's got to have money to find a job. Besides, he's earned the money I give him." Mary explained, "I feel sorry for him. He's so alone and so sad-looking. He doesn't have any friends or anything. He never seems to have any fun. I don't know, I just feel sorry for him."

Both Mary and Marty admitted that they found it hard to say no to Tim. Marty said he needed peace when he gets home from work, "not a raging maniac." Mary said Tim never got "really angry" with her the way he did with Marty, but "his words can hurt, you know. He says things that make me cry."

Both admitted that they spent much of their time trying to keep peace in their household.

Tim's violent behavior has increased over the years. He often shouts at his parents and Jenny, berates them viciously with foul language, throws plates of food on the floor, and engages in physical fights with Marty. Once he flung Marty to the floor and might have strangled him if Mary and Jenny had not intervened. Mary and Marty occasionally thought of calling the police but worried that a police record might hurt Tim's chances of getting a job. And they are ashamed, concerned about what their neighbors might think.

But now Mary and Marty are really scared—more scared than they've ever been. Tim has become paranoid. He thinks his parents are spying on him. And he thinks the FBI is sending poisonous vapors into their house via the telephone. "He ripped all the phones out last week," Mary told me. "We're afraid of what he might do next."

As well they should be. Tim's parents have been aware for quite some time that his chemical use has been causing gross deterioration in his personality. They have known for quite some time that he is in need of treatment, but they have been lulled into believing that they could not help Tim until he wanted help. Now, in the face of his apparent cocaine psychosis, they know they can wait no longer.

Most parents do discover a cause and effect relationship sooner or later, but as we have noted, many fail to see the chemical use as primary, or as the cause of their child's disintegrating behavior and personality. They believe that the chemical use is secondary, the result of the behavior/personality changes. So do many helping professionals to whom they turn. Such professionals do both parents and their children devastating disservice, as our case histories poignantly demonstrate.

Consider Sue. Her grades had fallen and she had moved up

to the third floor in her home, away from everyone. Sue had become sullen, noncommunicative, depressed. She seemed to lack self-confidence, saying she did not like herself anymore. So her parents trotted her off to a mental health therapist to be fixed up, but she got worse. She started to hang around with known users, stayed out past her curfew, came home drunk several times, and began to use foul language. Her parents upped her number of sessions each week with the therapist. The progressive, dangerous charade continued until the day Sue sat down outside the door to the alcohol/drug counselor's office at her school, took a razor blade out of her bookbag, and slashed her left wrist in one long, deep cut. She watched the blood flow for a few minutes, then tapped on the counselor's door (she knew he was in because she could hear voices) and waited to be rescued. Sue knew what kind of help she needed, even if no one else did.

Ned's case is another example of parents seeing an erroneous cause and effect relationship. His parents sent him to a psychiatrist for his depression, but Ned only became more depressed. His parents were not concerned that he drank beer, since all the kids Ned's age drank. They worried instead about the changes they were seeing: his alienation, his lack of motivation, what seemed like a deep sense of inadequacy, abrupt and unexplained mood swings, and insomnia. But mostly they were worried about his depression, which they never connected to his drinking. Neither did the psychiatrist.

One night, quite drunk, Ned drove into the garage, closed the garage doors, and kept the car engine running. His father found his body the next morning as he was leaving for work.

Then there is Brad, who was in psychotherapy for three years to address his emotional problems, but not his use of drugs. Barbara and John were told repeatedly that Brad would stop his abusive use of alcohol and other drugs once his emotional problems were resolved. They were also told repeatedly that they should be more understanding of Brad, more consistent in their parenting, less reactive, less rigid—more of this, less of that.

Throughout those three years Brad's emotional and behavioral problems got worse. So did his chemical use. And throughout the three years, Barbara and John became increasingly consumed by feelings of guilt and inadequacy. They actually came to believe they were at fault, the cause of Brad's problems.

Brad used chemicals from the time he was eleven until he was fifteen. These years encompass an important developmental stage, when children examine their own separateness and develop the kinds of skills that allow them to function independently. As we noted in Chapter 5, mind-altering drugs, including alcohol, impede this important maturation. Thus Brad missed out on the maturation that normally would have occurred. As a result, his recovery from chemical dependency has been horrendously difficult. And, now, at twenty-two, he is trying to begin what was not begun at eleven.

Brad's crucial developmental years need not have been wasted. Most likely they would not have been if Brad's chemical use had been considered primary, as the cause of his behavior/personality problems rather than as the result.

Don't misunderstand me: the majority of mental health professionals are honestly attempting to provide appropriate help for their clients. The problem lies not so much in their motivation as in their training. Unless a helping professional is specifically trained in dealing with chemical dependency, he cannot provide the help an adolescent user needs. You don't go to a heart specialist if you have food poisoning. Neither do you look to conventional psychotherapy—in any of its forms—for help with alcohol and other drug problems.

Although they may be highly trained in their specialties,

psychiatrists, psychologists, analysts, social workers, nurses, family counselors, and other therapists are ineffective in dealing with chemical dependency unless they've received additional specific training and education in chemical use issues. Addiction is a disease that threatens basic survival, and it needs to be treated that way—by a trained chemical dependency specialist.

If you suspect that your child is involved in harmful chemical use and you are trying to locate a helping professional for your son or daughter, how do you go about it? Check the appendix of this book for leads. You can also interview your local area mental health professionals, making sure to ask the following questions:

1. Do you believe that adolescents should use alcohol and other drugs? (If the answer is anything but an unequivocal no, head for the door.)
2. Do you have specific education and training in chemical dependency? If so, are you certified by your state as an alcohol-drug counselor? (If the answer to either question is no, look elsewhere.)
3. Do you insist that your clients participate in Narcotics Anonymous or Alcoholics Anonymous? (If the answer is no, again, head for the door.)

The answers to these questions—which should be asked near the beginning of any interview—will guide you in accurately assessing the professional's ability to help your teenager.

Conventional psychotherapy does play a very important role, but only with people motivated for personal growth and change—that is, people who are not chemically dependent. Adolescent users are not motivated for change; they're motivated for getting more drugs. Their defense mechanisms are so dense and their values so impaired by chemicals that their

KIDS, ALCOHOL & DRUGS

attitude is usually, "*You* shape up; then I'll be okay." Conventional psychotherapy is not equipped to deal with such an attitude and may even contribute to denial, rationalization, justification, and other defense mechanisms. It does not treat the chemical dependency as a disease, as primary.

Psychotherapy can be very valuable once kids get off alcohol and drugs. Although emotional problems may have contributed to chemical use, it is only after the teenager is clean and dry that it is possible to delve into the past experiences that have caused or contributed to his pain. Even then, many adolescents need to be stabilized in abstinence before they can deal with the chaotic feelings that will be unearthed by digging into the past.

Psychotherapy may ultimately help a teenager arrive at the root causes of his anguish, *but delving into the reasons for chemical use while an adolescent is still using is nothing less than insane.* If a raging fire were destroying your home, would you stand around, observing and analyzing the cause of the fire, figuring out whether it began in the basement or the kitchen? No. You'd call the fire department and put out the fire. Alcohol and other drug use is the fire that rages in chemically dependent adolescents. To save the life of your child, you have to put out the fire. Then perhaps its cause can be discovered.

There are few guarantees in life, but there is one in addition to death and taxes. If you have a child who repeatedly shows signs of chemical use and behavior/personality changes and you do not address the chemical use, *it is guaranteed that your child's behavior/personality problems will get worse.* You will be able to facilitate your child's recovery *only* if you consider the chemical use to be the cause of the behavior/personality changes. You will impede that recovery if you consider the behavior/personality changes to be the cause of the chemical use. It's as simple as that.

Responding appropriately by seeing the chemical cause and effect relationship requires three realizations. First, you must become a pragmatist. Realize that no matter the "reasons" cited for your teenager's chemical use, an adolescent should not be using alcohol and other drugs. Second, recognize that your child can't get well until he stops using alcohol and other drugs. Third, realize that if your child is addicted, he will not be able to stop using until he gets treatment specifically designed for chemically dependent adolescents.

The parents of Allison, Mark, and David were able to make the connection between their child's chemical use and the behavior/personality changes. They could also see that their child needed help in order to stop using chemicals. The parents of Joann, Ricky, Tim, and Brad eventually were able to reach these same conclusions.

Perhaps you, too, have reached these conclusions. If so, like the parents in this book, your next step is to determine which treatment best meets your child's needs.

How to Determine Treatment Needs

Adolescents who are harmfully involved with chemicals rarely realize it. Or, if they do, they rarely acknowledge the extent of their involvement. *Denial is a hallmark of addiction.*

A couple of winters ago I was rushing through New York's Grand Central Station when I was accosted—politely, but resolutely—by a young man waving an empty vodka bottle in my face. He was probably in his early twenties, but it was hard to tell; he was hidden behind long, shaggy hair and a beard, as well as innumerable layers of torn, filthy scarves, sweaters, jackets, and coats. Obviously one of New York's homeless, he told me he was an alcoholic in need of a drink and asked for money.

"No kidding, you're an alcoholic?" I was more curious than afraid, since his whole demeanor seemed friendly and polite.

"Yeah, bad. I got it bad. Can you give me some money?" he asked again.

"If you're an alcoholic, why don't you go to AA? There's a meeting right here in the station."

"AA? Jesus, lady!" he exclaimed, as his eyes nearly popped out of his head. "AA? Christ, I'm not that bad."

At the end of the addiction line, and he believed he was "not that bad."

Denial renders chemically dependent persons incapable of evaluating their condition with any degree of accuracy. Consequently, adolescents harmfully involved with alcohol and other drugs are not in a position to determine their own treatment needs. Their parents, and the professionals to whom they turn for help, will have to make such determinations for them. Parents may be able to offer their child a choice between two viable options, but it is the parents themselves who should select those options.

Although several important guidelines exist for determining which treatment option, or combination of options, is most appropriate for a particular adolescent, I cannot emphasize enough the need for parents to work in conjunction with professionals specialized in addiction. Not only are these specialists familiar with the various treatment options, but they are also skilled in helping parents secure their child's cooperation. In addition, because of their education, training, and experience in the chemical dependency field, the specialists are in a position to know more about the child's treatment needs than parents can be expected to know.

The safest posture parents can take during the process of treatment selection is to think in terms of *more* treatment, not less. Not surprisingly, parents have a strong need to minimize the seriousness of their child's condition. But while less treatment may make them feel better, it seldom fulfills their child's actual needs.

Addiction is an incredibly powerful phenomenon. Remember the hold addiction has on a child. The urge to get high— to feel a chemical's effect—is automatic, coming and going of its own accord, even if the child is no longer using. When the urge strikes, it will feel overwhelming; satisfying the urge will seem more important than anything else in the child's life.

Consequently, for the safety of the child, I reiterate: parents should always think in terms of more treatment, not less.

How to Determine
Your Child's Treatment Needs

Follow these four criteria to determine what type of treatment your child needs: (1) the extensiveness of chemical use, including the type of chemical and the duration, amount, and frequency of use; (2) the degree of control over behavior; (3) the willingness to cooperate; and (4) the extent of denial.

First, extensiveness of use is often difficult for parents to evaluate. Usually only an addiction specialist can get through the lying, discrepancies, minimizing, maximizing, omissions, and other maneuvers kids pull in their attempts to hide their history of chemical use.

To help you gather clues about the types of chemicals an adolescent may be using (and in what combinations), as well as the length of time, dosage, and frequency with which he may have been using them, study chapters 5 and 8. Remember, however, that only a trained chemical dependency specialist can accurately assess these variables.

Heavy use, culminating in late-stage addiction, is unmistakably revealed by the presence of withdrawal symptoms, which require medically supervised detoxification. Withdrawal, particularly from alcohol and other central nervous system depressants, can be so painful that an adolescent may be virtually compelled to give up and start using again unless he has both medical supervision and detoxifying agents. *It can also be fatal.* The presence *of any withdrawal symptoms*—paralyzing lethargy, profound depression, extreme agitation, seizures, shaking, dry heaves, or severe abdominal cramps—usually necessitates treatment in an in-patient setting, no matter what the other three criteria for determining treatment needs indicate.

Second, the amount of control a child has over his own behavior is an excellent indicator of a child's treatment needs. Those who have lost significant control will require a highly controlled treatment environment, no matter what the other three criteria indicate. An adolescent with a good measure of control may be suited to a less structured, out-patient treatment facility; again, it depends upon your assessment of the other variables.

How do you assess degree of control over behavior? By using a highly objective yardstick: Is your son or daughter following your household rules or not? Very simply, does he get up in time to go to school? Does she do her assigned chores? Does he keep curfews? Is she doing what she is asked? If so, then your adolescent is in control of his behavior. If your child is not following household, school, or societal rules, if classes are cut, school rules are broken, abusive language is used, violence breaks out, and/or curfews are broken, then he is not in charge of his behavior.

Third, the degree of denial a child exhibits is an excellent indicator of his treatment needs. If he insists that chemicals are not a problem, that he can stop using any time he wishes, the child is *not* a good candidate for self-help groups, since the effectiveness of these groups is based on the user's acknowledging his loss of control over chemical use. If, on the other hand, the child readily admits to having no control over chemical use, self-help groups might be a viable treatment option.

Denial usually goes hand in hand with the fourth indicator, the degree of willingness to cooperate. Generally, *the greater the denial, the greater the lack of willingness to cooperate*, both of which point to a need for residential treatment.

To one degree or another, most children who are harmfully involved with chemicals show both denial and an unwillingness to cooperate. Believing that everyone else is crazy while they are sane, they maintain that their chemical use is no different from anyone else's. Consequently, most feel no need for treatment and are unwilling to go along with it. There are exceptions, of course—those kids who will admit they have a problem, plead for help, and be willing to do anything asked of them.

It is the different way these four factors combine that determines which type of treatment is most appropriate. A child who manifests a high degree of all four variables requires the most structured, comprehensive treatment available. On the other hand, a child whose willingness to cooperate is exemplary and whose drug use is moderate might do very well in out-patient treatment, even if the degree of denial is high, so long as the child has not shown a significant loss of control over his own behavior.

Let's look at the chemically involved children we have been following and assess their treatment needs according to the four criteria we've discussed: extensiveness of use, control over behavior, willingness to cooperate, and degree of denial. Since Ricky, Brad, JoAnn, and Tim are the most harmfully involved, their treatment needs are the most easily discernible. They all have severe chemical use histories, though only two show withdrawal symptoms. Ricky has had extreme abdominal cramps in the absence of heroin, and JoAnn has experienced a paralyzing lethargy following a suspected crack binge. All four show significant loss of control over behavior. None show any willingness to cooperate, and all appear heavily entrenched in denial. (Ricky did admit to the use of heroin when I first saw him but denied he was addicted, despite the presence of withdrawal symptoms.) All should be candidates for residential treatment.

Allison and Mark show a moderate use of chemicals, and David shows an even milder use, as he demonstrates considerable control over his behavior by following most rules at home and at school. Mark's suspension and expulsion from schools show some loss of control, but he still follows most standards of behavior. Allison, on the other hand, has been showing a moderate amount of loss of control over her behavior both at home and at school. Both David and Allison seem heavily entrenched in denial, while Mark admits to being addicted. If they are willing to cooperate (which remains to be seen), all are candidates for some sort of out-patient treatment program.

Treatment Facilities

Until recently there were no treatment facilities specifically designed for chemically dependent adolescents. Only within recent years has adolescent treatment become a specialty, based on the recognition that teenagers need alternatives to adult treatment models. Fortunately, there are now a number of treatment options available to adolescents suffering harmful chemical involvements. They include self-help groups (Alcoholics Anonymous, Narcotics Anonymous, Cocaine Anonymous); out-patient clinics, agencies, and private practitioners designed for individual and group therapy; comprehensive out-patient chemical dependency centers (where the child lives at home but spends his days and evenings at the center); comprehensive four- to six-week in-patient chemical dependency centers; halfway houses used following in-patient chemical dependency centers for three to twelve months; psychiatric hospitals that have separate chemical dependency units for treating adolescents with duo-disorders (serious psychiatric illnesses plus chemical dependency); and one- to two-year residential drug centers, often called therapeutic communities. While treatment varies in intensity, structure, and comprehensiveness, all these options have one thing in common: *treatment is predicated on abstinence from addictive chemicals.*

Adolescent chemical dependency treatment has become sophisticated. Upon admission to an in-patient chemical dependency treatment center, the child is given a medical examination and then, under medical supervision, is withdrawn from all drugs. If needed, special drugs are given to ensure that withdrawal will be as safe and as comfortable as possible. Once the child is chemically free, his chemical history is evaluated. Psychological tests are then given to determine the presence and extent of addiction, as well as possible underlying disorders, such as depression. If the child is found to be addicted, an individual treatment plan is developed that meets his specific needs. Psychiatric therapy may be necessary or an antidepressant drug may be prescribed. (*Antidepressant and antipsychotic drugs are not addicting* and therefore can be safely administered to the chemically dependent children who need them. Most adolescents, once chemically free, are not seriously depressed or psychotic, and thus do not need such drugs.) The treatment plan also meets general needs by providing group therapy, individual counseling, lectures, reading and writing assignments, physical workouts, and schooling, so that the child need not fall behind academically while in treatment.

Selecting a Treatment Program for Your Child

You should follow these criteria when selecting the appropriate treatment program for your adolescent: (1) the availability of treatment, (2) the nature of the home environment, (3) the transitional nature of adolescence, (4) the cost of treatment, (5) the quality of treatment, and (6) the success rate of the program.

One of the primary considerations for any parent choosing a program is the availability of treatment. Self-help groups and out-patient individual and group counseling services exist in most areas of the United States. The four- to six-week comprehensive residential chemical dependency treatment centers are fewer in number and therefore may not be conveniently located. Nevertheless, such centers are residential, so travel is required only at the beginning and end of treatment. Halfway houses (often called extended-care facilities), used in conjunction with the four- to six-week centers, are fewer in number, and many children in need may be unable to find one. Comprehensive out-patient treatment centers are scarce, and many candidates for such care must settle for residential treatment. Long-term residential treatment facilities or therapeutic communities exist in several areas of the country, but, largely because of the recent increase in crack addiction, many have long waiting lists. Generally speaking, the private four- to six-week chemical dependency centers for those covered by insurance or who can pay do not have long waiting lists; those therapeutic communities that are publically funded often do.

The nature of the adolescent's home environment is another determinant in choosing an appropriate treatment program. Many addicted children have an addicted parent whose chemical use is counterproductive to the child's recovery. A number of parents who were teenagers in the sixties still feel that marijuana is a "safe" drug and may unwittingly contribute to their child's return to chemical use. Other children have abusive parents, or parents otherwise unwilling or unable to provide a setting conducive to recovery. As we will see in Chapter 10, the dysfunction present in many homes virtually requires that some teenagers who might otherwise have qualified for out-patient treatment be removed from the family environment for treatment. Although many parents feel that they are abandoning their children if they send them to a residential center, this option is in fact the best one if the previously mentioned circumstances prevail. It allows both parents and children to get the help they each need and to begin building the foundation for a new, healthy family structure.

The transitional nature of adolescence can also be a factor

in determining a treatment option. A college-bound high school senior, for example, might not be a good candidate for out-patient treatment simply because he will not be around long enough to complete it. In this case, the more comprehensive but shorter-term residential treatment setting is preferable.

Cost is also an essential factor. Many treatment options are surprisingly affordable. Self-help groups are, of course, free. Members can chip in to help defray costs of refreshments and rent if they wish, but that's all. And out-patient counseling rarely presents a financial problem. In many areas federally and state-funded clinics are available for those without insurance or other financial means. Private clinics, agencies, and practitioners are also readily available in most areas, and usually accept third-party payments or have a sliding-fee scale. (All are listed in local telephone directories.)

The four- to six-week adolescent chemical dependency treatment centers, where treatment is provided by highly trained professionals and which incorporate, among other things, the Twelve Step program of Alcoholics Anonymous, are considered by many to be "state of the art" in their quality of services. Unfortunately, they are available only to children who have insurance coverage or to those who can pay in full. The same holds true for most of the halfway houses or extended-care facilities, which many adolescents need following the short-term chemical dependency treatment. Luckily, many of the long-term therapeutic communities, where treatment is provided in large part by nonprofessional recovering addicts supervised by trained professionals, are federally and state funded and thus can treat adolescents not covered by insurance or parental funding. As I've mentioned, however, admission often requires lengthy waits. (Federally and state-funded facilities are listed in local telephone directories, as are most of the privately funded facilities. Please also see the appendices in the back of this book.)

Although you may feel totally incompetent when it comes to determining the quality of treatment programs, there are trustworthy resources to help you, especially these two books: *The 100 Best Treatment Centers in the United States*, by Linda Sunshine and John Wright, and *Rehab*, by Stan Hart (see the bibliography). In each, centers across the United States are evaluated according to type of treatment provided, physical facilities, philosophy, cost, types of insurance accepted, admissions policy, staff qualifications, special programs, family involvement, and aftercare. While these books describe adult treatment centers, they include those centers that also have adolescent treatment units. The appendices and bibliography at the end of this book also list resources that can help you assess the quality of existing programs.

There are components you as a parent can use to determine quality of treatment programs. First, all quality programs take a holistic approach to chemical dependency treatment, recognizing that the disease is threefold—physical, psychological, and spiritual. From providing medical detoxification to physical exercise, from ensuring proper nutrition to teaching stress-reduction techniques, a comprehensive program addresses an adolescent's physical needs. The treatment offered by sophisticated, highly trained, and credentialed staff members (no more than 50 percent should be recovering addicts) via group therapy, individual counseling, a family program, lectures, audiovisual presentations, psychodrama, assertiveness training, and other such activities should meet a teenager's psychological needs. And the best means of addressing an adolescent's spiritual needs is through respect, loving care, and the Twelve Step program of Alcoholics Anonymous (as well as Cocaine Anonymous and Narcotics Anonymous), all of which are an integral part of the most successful treatment programs.

A word of caution: Programs should *never* use shame-based tactics, such as "hot seat" pychic bashings and signs worn around the neck proclaiming the adolescent to be a "horse's ass." Addiction is degrading enough; chemically dependent adolescents do not need treatment that degrades them further. I would also advise you to stay away from programs that use methadone maintenance. Frequently used to wean addicts off of heroin, this medically approved synthetic drug shows a success rate of only about 10 percent. Moreover, it merely allows the adolescent to substitute one drug for another, without addressing the addiction itself and providing the motivation to become chemical-free.

The following list will help you ask the right questions as you look for an appropriate treatment program for your child:

1. Is the program based on total abstinence from alcohol and other drugs?
2. What is the recovery rate of the program? (Some programs have a high dropout rate and base their recovery rate only on those who complete the program. Therefore, also ask about the dropout rate.)
3. What are the staff's credentials?
4. What is the counselor/client ratio?
5. Does the program make use of or advocate the Twelve Step program?
6. Is there a program of family involvement?
7. Is there preparation for aftercare?
8. Are the educational programs certified by the state?
9. What is the background and history of the treatment center?
10. Is the center accredited by the Joint Commission on Accreditation of Hospitals, and is the program licensed by the state?
11. Are shame-based tactics ever employed?
12. Is methadone maintenance advocated?
13. Is detoxification provided?

14. Is the facility affiliated with a hospital if it is a freestanding unit?
15. Does the program address the physical, psychological, and spiritual needs of its clients?
16. What is the cost of the program?
17. What types of insurance does the program accept? Does the program offer alternative financial arrangements if needed?

The last variable is the success rate of the program. Although not all programs have conducted up-to-date studies of their individual success rates, some verifiable data ought to be available. Generally, good programs average a success rate of approximately 65 percent. You should be suspicious of recovery rates that are either considerably lower or considerably higher than this figure.

Getting treatment, even the best treatment at the most comprehensive, high-quality center, does not guarantee that your adolescent will recover from chemical dependency—but not getting treatment is a virtual guarantee that your child will not recover. Treatment is the only hope you've both got. Get it!

TEN

Parental Codependency

We have looked at what happens to children who develop harmful chemical involvements, and we've started to examine how to address their needs. Now we must look at what happens to their parents, who suffer enormously. Parents need and deserve help—for their own sake, as well as for the sake of their chemically dependent adolescents.

When Allison began to exhibit changes in her personality, Phyllis was on her case day and night. Becoming Allison's "snoopervisor," she checked out all her friends, and all her tapes and records, forbidding some, permitting others. She checked Allison's homework. She visited Allison's school every few weeks to check on her progress and behavior. While she remained willing to incur Allison's wrath, she nonetheless found herself becoming dependent upon Allison's good moods in order to feel good herself.

Stuart, normally an active participant in family life, had a very different reaction from Phyllis. He started to withdraw. He kept wanting Phyllis to back off Allison's case. He hated to go home at the end of the workday, knowing he would have to hear of Allison's behavior. Once home, he hid behind his computer, yet thoughts about Allison kept constantly creeping, unbeckoned, into his head.

Are their reactions so unusual? No, they're not; that's the whole point. Anyone of us, as loving parents, would do similar things. A year later, when nothing seemed to work, both parents became more controlling. Phyllis barraged Allison daily with questions, demanding to know what Allison thought, felt, and did throughout her entire day. Stuart scoured the papers to find movies to go to on weekend evenings, ostensibly so that the family could all have fun together, but really so he could keep Allison away from her older "troubled" peers.

Intent—very intent—upon getting Allison fixed up, Phyllis and Stuart were greatly disappointed to find that Allison's new school was not the answer. Tortured because they could not make Allison happy, they came to believe her emotional well-being was their responsibility. Phyllis began to feel that she couldn't do anything right, that she was failing as a parent. Stuart felt that he could do nothing to please, and began to think there was something wrong with him as both a parent and a husband.

When asked what she wanted for her birthday, Melissa, their other child, requested "just one meal where you don't talk about Allison all the time." Phyllis and Stuart were allowing Allison to take over their lives. They no longer focused on their own reasonable self-interests, nor on those of the family. They no longer felt as loving toward each other, and had stopped being actively engaged with friends and community events. And they didn't really know or seem to care very much about Melissa, who just kept to herself.

Won't all this stop, once Allison gets well? Won't Phyllis and Stuart get back to normal once Allison is normal?

Maybe. It all depends on how habituated they have become to their maladaptive responses, how set they have become in their new ways. While Phyllis and Stuart will most likely have trouble letting go of Allison so she can assume responsibility for her own recovery, both are aware of the changes they have made, which they know are not normal. They remember the way they used to be and don't like the way they have become—all of which indicates their treatment requirements probably will not be great.

Mary and Marty are much more deeply entrenched than Phyllis and Stuart. In their case, they could recall how Tim used to be, but not how they felt and acted before Tim's problems dominated their lives. They admit that their lives are full of problems, but they firmly believe Tim is the only cause. All would be well, if only Tim would get well.

Mary worked as a dental hygienist an hour away from home. Marty worked close to thirteen hours a day, six days a week, in his dry-cleaning store. Both worked hard at their jobs and at keeping their home maintained. And both worked hard trying to cope with Tim.

Mary looked like a dental hygienist should look—friendly, neat, a little more scattered than one might wish, but competent, probing, thorough, and caring. She was attractive, effusive, and somewhat matronly. One could easily picture her, if not cleaning teeth, then cooking huge holiday dinners while talking nonstop. She'd had a brief affair with one of the dentists in her office a couple of years back and still felt enormously guilty. Currently, she misses a day or two of work just about every month due to "overwhelming" migraines.

"I've made myself sick worrying about Tim," she admitted. Sometimes she feels like she is going crazy. "I forget things. I can't concentrate anymore, and sometimes I just go blank. Last Saturday I was driving to the supermarket but ended up at my office, and I don't even know how I got there. I mean, I know I was driving, but I don't remember it, and that's close to an hour of driving. And I can't make decisions anymore. Even little decisions . . . like which brand of orange juice to buy.'' Mary also admitted that she has often wished "everything was over.'' When questioned further, she said that many times she wished she could die—"get it over with"—but denied any specific plans for carrying out that wish.

Marty weighed close to 300 pounds, held himself aloof, and was often hostile in manner—all in all, quite forbidding. He hadn't had sex with Mary, or apparently anyone, for several years, but he acted as if that were irrelevant. "I'm not here to talk about my sex life,'' he told me. He does not believe he has an eating disorder. He attributes his weight gain to working next door to a pizza parlor. He is a man of few words and is hard to get close to.

In their reactions to Tim, it was not clear who pursued and who distanced; both seemed to do a lot of switching back and forth. Both worried endlessly. Both were incredibly controlling and deeply entrenched in a caretaking relationship with Tim. They parceled out daily and weekly allowances, which they knew would be spent on drugs. Marty insisted on paying Tim's car insurance premiums because "he'll need a car to find a job.'' They refused to call the police when Tim became violent because a police record might interfere with Tim's chances of getting a job. Mary cleaned Tim's room each week so he would not live in "squalor.'' Marty dragged Tim into the shower several times each week and then watched to make sure he actually took a shower. "Once I found him sitting on the john with the shower on. He's a sneak; you have to watch his every move.'' Mary listened in on Tim's phone calls. Marty read his mail. Mary fixed special meals, which she carried into Tim's room on a "neat little tray with legs'' purchased for that purpose. Marty insisted that Tim eat at the table "with the rest of us.'' The fact that Tim refused to eat at either setting seemed to elude them. And on it went for years, with each endlessly obsessing, controlling, and fixing.

■ ■

How, you might be asking, can parents let something like this go on for so long? Easy.

Being overcome by addiction in someone you love is easy—terribly easy. For when a child starts losing control of his chemical use, and consequently, of his behavior, anarchy starts to reign in the household. Rules are broken. Limits are discarded. Standards of behavior go by the wayside. The longer a child remains trapped in harmful chemical involvement, the greater the breakdown of authority. In time, parents end up abdicating their authoritative role, and the child does whatever he wishes.

As a result of this breakdown within the household, some very painful and destructive parental responses become the norm, responses that reflect a condition known as *codependency*. Codependent parents allow their addicted child to affect them so profoundly that they are consumed by their child's behavior. Codependents usually live according to unwritten rules that are governing their behavior without their realizing it. These rules forbid the expression of feelings, trust in oneself and in others, playfulness, honest communication, realistic goals and expectations, and self-care.

Let's examine the origins of parental codependency. It is when the addictive process escalates and the chemically dependent adolescent's behavior deteriorates so much that parents try desperately to control their child's decisions, feelings, and behavior. They try to ''fix'' their child, becoming compelled to do for their child what in fact the child should do for himself. They begin to focus obsessively on the child, losing sight of themselves, each other, and their other children. Their lives become increasingly unmanageable.

Ironically, the more out of control the chemically dependent adolescent becomes, the more controlling, coercive, and manipulative the parents become. Because all external behavioral guidelines have broken down, the parents themselves become stand-ins for the rules, creating a situation that generates increasingly distorted parental behavior. Life becomes a massive power struggle. Each side—with the parents often pitted against each other—becomes obsessed with winning. Minor wins are followed by major losses. Ultimately, of course, no one in a power struggle wins. As we will see in Chapter 11, when clearly articulated rules exist in a family, and the consequences of not following these rules are known and enforced, then parents can sit back and relax. They don't have to interfere and control.

In a healthy family environment, children are emotionally dependent on their parents who are responsible *to* them for support, nurturance, and affirmation. In a family with a chemically dependent adolescent, the parents become emotionally dependent on the adolescent and responsible *for* him. They come to believe that they can't feel good if their child doesn't. They don't make a move regarding their child until they have figured out how their child will react. Such perpetual "walking on eggs" eventually paralyzes the whole family unit, keeping everyone except the addicted child on tenterhooks.

As we have seen, chemical dependency is powerful. It makes very different children become alike, so alike that they start doing the same kinds of things. Codependency is equally powerful, making very different parents come to behave in a similar way. You can take very different families, place a chemically dependent teenager in them, and those families will eventually display the same warped behavioral patterns.

You may breathe a sigh of relief as you read about some of the parents in this book, telling yourself, "Well, at least I haven't done that." Perhaps you haven't slugged your child, or been attacked by her. Maybe you haven't run out to get booze or drugs for your son, or desperately searched every known hangout in town for your missing daughter. Maybe you haven't given her money that you know will be used for drugs, or bailed him out of jail in the middle of the night.

Perhaps you haven't locked your child in one night, out the next. Maybe you haven't done any of these things; *but if your child remains harmfully involved with chemicals, and you don't get help for yourself, start thinking in terms of "yet."* Chemical dependency is progressive, *and so is codependency.* No one is immune. Without help, the more deviant our child becomes, the less rationally we act. Codependency starts out as a normal response to an abnormal situation. The problem is, the normal response eventually becomes a maladaptive response, destructive to self and others. Guaranteed!

As the addiction progresses, the chemically dependent child becomes expert at producing feelings of guilt in the parents. Even under the best of conditions, young teenagers have problems assuming responsibility for their own behavior. Eleven- to fifteen-year-old kids are projectors; they blame everyone but themselves for their behavior. Unlike other adolescents, chemically dependent adolescents do not grow out of this stage; in fact, they become immersed in it. As their illness progresses, they become increasingly unwilling and unable to accept responsibility for their own actions.

Their parents, in turn, begin to accept the blame. If blamed forcefully enough for a long enough time, even the strongest parent will begin to feel at fault. I have yet to meet a parent who has not, to one degree or another, felt responsible for his chemically dependent child's irresponsible behavior.

When they fail time and again in the face of ever-increasing problems, parents suffer marked losses of self-esteem. Frustrated, angry, and guilty, they become even more compelled to control and fix, thus establishing a downward spiral of behavior. Since nothing is working, the parents are destined to suffer a growing loss of self-esteem and become increasingly emotionally dependent upon the ups and downs of their child.

The subject of the chemically dependent child consumes the parents' energy, until they lose themselves so completely that their child's moods and behavior control their own. When the child acts, they react. They spend hours planning what they are going to say or do to their child, mentally rehearsing all day long. They become obsessed with the idea of finding the one plan that will reach their child, the one approach that will make him change. Parents of a chemically dependent child can recite in great detail what their child thinks, feels, and does; that is, what they *assume* their child thinks, feels, and does. In time, it's hard to tell where child ends and parent begins.

Of the two parents, one is usually the pursuer, who keeps on the child's case all the time, and the other the distancer, who goes to great lengths to avoid dealing with the child's problems. At first glance, it often looks as if the pursuer is more emotionally involved with the child. In fact, it takes as much psychic energy to avoid as it does to engage. It is also important to realize that the distancer can alienate himself only because the pursuer is so actively involved. Once the pursuer stops, the distancer moves in like lightning to the rod. The two attitudes are really sides of the same coin.

This issue of pursuing and distancing responses is capable of shattering the marriage. Each parent's obsessive child-focus leaves little energy for self or spouse, causing estrangement. At the same time, the conflicting responses cause a great deal of animosity. Given sufficient estrangement and animosity, it is not uncommon for one partner to begin thinking about ways to get out.

The chemically dependent child also negatively affects the entire family system. A dysfunctional family (like a codependent person) follows a very strong set of rigid, crazy-making rules that, because they are never articulated, gain in power. If the rules of a dysfunctional family were actually written out and posted on the refrigerator, no one would follow them. Such rules include: don't share your feelings; don't laugh and play; take everything very seriously; don't meet your own valid needs; beware of intimacy; ignore problems; and, at all costs, don't upset the chemically dependent child. Following such rules makes everyone act in dysfunctional ways.

The parent's degree of codependency will be significantly less if the child's chemical dependency has been recognized and treated early. The codependency, and resulting dysfunction, is also reduced if, in addition, the parent did not develop codependency early in life in response to dysfunction in his own parents.

All of this is why I am encouraging you so strongly to get help *as soon as you see* some of the behavior/personality changes in your child. You, and your family as a whole, might easily be overcome by this illness.

In addition to the inherent power of chemical dependency, which virtually demands a maladaptive response, any number of other factors can contribute to a codependent response. Like Mary and Marty, many of us have been parenting for years. By the time a troubled child comes along, we might lack the parenting energies we once had. Then, too, the troubled child might come along at a time when we are taking a good hard look at our lives, and asking, ''Is this it?'' We may trap ourselves in a job we hate, so that we can get the pension, or because college expenses for our children are just beginning. Or we might find our marriage diminishing, rather than deepening. The truth is that when an addicted child comes along, demanding heroic, greater-than-normal parental responses, our energies for just plain parenting may have been preempted.

We may miss doing what needs to be done simply because we don't see it. Human nature being what it is, we cannot see things clearly when we are in the midst of all the action. This phenomenon of cloudy vision was brought home to me several years ago, albeit in a far milder form. I had lived in the heart of Manhattan for many years and had always felt perfectly safe. Then I lived in Atlanta for one year, during which time I read repeatedly about all the terrible things that were going on in Manhattan—the muggings, rapes, murders, and so on. Over the course of the year—despite the fact that my then husband, unscathed in New York, was mugged in Atlanta—I started becoming fearful of Manhattan. Yet once back in New York, the crime situation again seemed normal to me.

As horrible as it may actually be, living with an addicted child does not seem nearly as bad as reading about it, or watching it on television, or seeing it in someone else's family. What in actuality is aberrant begins to seem normal to those involved. It is only with outside input, or some emotional or physical distance, that you can have clarity of vision. Mary and Marty had no outside input, and since they were much too close, their vision was, indeed, cloudy.

No matter how accurately recorded, any case history is distorted by what is left out. Dramatic events get mentioned, while more mundane events go unrecorded, although they may share in impact. In Tim's case, all the peaceful periods, the good times, go unmentioned. So are all the times when Tim seemed to shape up—the days, even weeks, when he actually looked good and behaved well. Each time Mary and Mary would become hopeful, only to have their hopes dashed. With addiction, both the good and the bad times are ultimately equally draining.

Victimizers don't believe in words, but victims do. Both parents, Marty especially, frequently used the words "I told him," as if the spoken words had power. "I told him if he smoked pot at my shop, I'd call the police." "I told him he had to get a job." "I told him to shape up or ship out." "I told him." "I told him." "I told him." Mary and Marty had become so victimized by Tim's addiction that they had lost their ability to put their words into action. They came to depend totally on Tim to effect change.

Instead of responding to such abuse with feelings of anger, many parents, like Mary, feel sad and cry. Or, like Marty, they deny anger but fly off into frustrated, impotent rages. Either way, when they remain largely out of touch with their anger, they do not have access to its energy, and thus feel impotent and powerless.

The pain that comes with loving a chemically dependent child is profound. Marty surrounded himself with an aura of hostility to keep himself from any more hurt. Mary protected herself by being busy, busy, busy. The pain that comes with responding codependently is also profound, so profound that lives become unmanageable. Mary and Marty had lost control of themselves; their thinking had become obsessive, their feelings predominantly negative, and their behavior compulsive. They suffered serious medical problems. Their marriage was about as estranged as marriages can be. No longer perceiving themselves as separate, worthy individuals, they had become adjuncts to Tim.

Their recovery does not rest upon Tim, no matter how much Mary and Marty believe it does. Codependency does not go away, especially codependency of this magnitude. Once you've got it, you've got it. Unless Mary and Marty get help for themselves, they will stay sick, no matter what Tim does or does not do.

Before parents can begin to help their chemically dependent child, they have to see that, despite their best intentions, their codependent behavior—their obsessing, controlling, fixing, and child-focus—have hurt, not helped, both themselves and their child. Before they can change, they must acknowledge what needs to be changed.

Self-help groups—Al-Anon, Families Anonymous, and Toughlove—do educate those who attend their meetings, but they offer much more besides: support, faith, strength, hope, and love. Hospitals, chemical dependency treatment centers, and alcohol/drug agencies offer seminars, workshops, and lectures on codependency and chemical dependency. Books, pamphlets, and magazines, many of which are listed at the end of this book, are available for helping codependent parents.

Next, parents need to seek codependency counseling. In order to get well, they must become *disengaged*. They must "let go" of their child, which, of course, is easier said than done. But it *is* possible. With knowledge, support from others who have been there, and professional counseling, parents can help themselves and their child.

Moderately codependent parents, like Phyllis and Stuart, can often help themselves and their using teenager at the same time. But parents like Mary and Marty, who have lived with chemical dependency for a long time and paid the consequences, are so devastated by the disease that they cannot even begin to help their child until they have first sought help for themselves.

Although many people believe that family therapy can help parents with a chemically dependent child, unless the therapy addresses the issues of chemical dependency and codependency, it will *not* help. Just as we noted in Chapter 8 that conventional psychotherapy is not designed to help a chemically dependent person until he is stabilized in abstinence from all mood-altering chemicals, so conventional family therapy is not designed to help the codependent family until the family has addressed its enabling issues in a program designed for that purpose. The power of codependency is stronger than that of conventional therapy. You must have enough respect for the disease to respond with specifically designed treatment.

How to Help Kids Who Agree to Cooperate

As we mature, most of us internalize a measure of discipline, which, in its turn, helps us to travel life's path successfully. We incorporate, or take into ourselves, this kind of discipline from role models—parents, teachers, and other authority figures—and from living in accordance with the necessary rules, regulations, and guidelines in our environment. But some teenagers never develop the inner discipline necessary for self-control and self-mastery, perhaps because they never had appropriate role models or consistent and rational rules. In other instances, adolescents did internalize discipline, but that discipline was then destroyed (as are values) by chemical dependency.

Adolescents like Allison, who consistently break some of the established family rules, show a loss of discipline. Such teenagers need to live in a structured, controlled environment until they learn to incorporate its rules, either for the first time (if never learned) or for the second time (if destroyed by chemical dependency). Adolescents like Allison need guidelines clearly stated and modeled so they can internalize and live by them. Thus, if they remain at home, their treatment should be based on rules of behavior that are *written out*. In this way, everyone—parents, child, and counselors—knows exactly what is expected. Adolescents like Mark and David, who follow most rules in their homes and schools, usually do not need rules that are written out.

Whether written or not, the clearly stated rules constitute a "contract" to be used with cooperative adolescents. The contract includes both nonnegotiable and negotiable rules. (A sample contract appears on page 154.) The nonnegotiable rules involve no alcohol and other drug use, no verbal or physical violence, and no skipping of classes. The rules you can negotiate with your child should cover school performance, personal cleanliness, curfews, and household chores. Privileges—including living at home, going out in the evenings, using the telephone and car, and participating in after-school activities and sports—can be earned if the child follows the rules of the contract *in full*. Conversely, the privileges are withdrawn if the rules are broken.

The consequences of breaching the contract should be as clearly stated as the rules themselves. Children who are unwilling up front to follow both nonnegotiable and negotiable rules lose the right to live at home. They *must* be admitted to a residential treatment facility. Children who enter into the contract but then use alcohol or other drugs must be admitted to a residential facility or receive more extensive out-patient treatment (whichever was agreed upon in the contract). Children who abstain from chemical use but break other rules lose such privileges as evenings out, telephone and car use, or participation in extracurricular activities. If they repeatedly break these other rules two weeks in a row, they lose the privilege of living at home and must be admitted to a residential treatment facility.

The contract creates the controlled environment needed by adolescents who are harmfully involved with chemicals. Without it, treatment cannot even begin. The contract gives children the opportunity to prove they are not addicted or to take their treatment seriously. It allows adolescents to develop trust in a structured, stable, predictable, outer environment and in the inner discipline they are learning. The contract gives children the opportunity to be responsible for their own behavior, to know in advance what the consequences will be for their behavior, and to make rational choices.

The contract also gives parents the opportunity to let go. Instead of controlling or fixing, they can back off and let their child function within the contract's controlled environment. It also helps parents to determine if their child needs more treatment and/or another environment.

But children respect and follow the contract if, *and only if*, their parents do. Severely codependent parents tend to have difficulty abiding by the contract. Instead of backing off, they continue to be on their child's case, virtually guaranteeing their child's rebellion. Or they might distance themselves so completely that they fail to monitor their child's behavior and do not know when consequences need to be imposed. Many do not even enforce the stated consequences when they know the rules of the contract have been broken. Parents who know they will not be able to follow the contract should not even consider having their child live at home. His life may literally depend on following the agreement. Instead, they should seek help in getting their child into a residential facility and begin working on their own illness.

Parents who are codependent to a lesser degree do honor the contract, but most need help in abiding by it. By their very nature adolescents will test the contract over and over and over. Parents, being parents, will be tempted to nag, pointing out how the contract should and should not be followed; or they will be tempted to give in and let the child get away with breaking the rules. Outside help, whether from self-help groups or professional codependency counseling, will give them the necessary strength to let the contract work as it is supposed to. Parents will then be able to let the child decide whether to follow or break it, and, based on their child's actions, impose the consequences.

Once the basic nonnegotiable and negotiable rules have been established, parents can put together an agreed-upon treatment plan designed to meet the needs of the child's specific harmful chemical involvement. Examples of such plans follow later in the chapter. If it ends up that your child is addicted, he can use Alcoholics Anonymous or Narcotics Anonymous or Cocaine Anonymous as a treatment base, and add a recovery support group or individual therapy based on chemical abstinence for further assistance. If available or warranted, the child could enter a comprehensive out-patient treatment facility.

If addiction is suspected but not established, have your child attend chemical dependency information classes at school or at local agencies. If such classes are not available, have your child attend weekly AA Beginner's meetings. Additionally, the child should receive therapy from private practitioners who are knowledgeable about chemical dependency and who recognize the child's need for abstinence from all mood-altering chemicals.

If the signs of chemical use and behavior/personality changes are few in number and the child heeds the contract, no additional treatment may be required.

Allison's parents were initially unsure about which path to take. They had considered psychotherapy, but not only did Allison talk them out of it, they were not convinced psychotherapy was the right direction. Allison had everything going for her—lots of strong personal resources, no handicaps, and a healthy family environment, almost right up to the point at which her parents became aware of her drinking. Phyllis and Stuart became more certain as time went on that Allison's drinking was causing her behavior/personality changes, and so they were receptive to having Allison's alcohol use evaluated.

Let's pick up where we left off—toward the end of the session at which I took Allison's alcohol/drug history.

"Allison, make my day. Tell me you know you are addicted and want treatment," I suggested.

"But I'm not addicted and I don't want treatment," she answered with a trace of defiance. She was scared to death, trying bravely to hide her feelings.

"That's what I figured you'd say. Listen, something's got to be done. You just can't be allowed to go on like this."

"But I stopped drinking and I'm not addicted," Allison insisted. "You can't prove I'm addicted. You just said you can't." This kid was a fighter, spunky and persistent, with a demeanor that belied her years.

"That's interesting, Allison. The way I see it, it isn't up to me or your parents to prove you are addicted. You're the one who's been drinking, so it's up to *you* to prove you're not addicted."

"What do you mean?"

"Well, one option we might consider is drawing up a contract that would govern both your alcohol use and your behavior. Want to hear about it?"

"Not especially," Allison answered forthrightly.

"Well, I'm going to tell you about it anyway. You would agree not to use alcohol in any form or any other drugs, and if you broke your agreement, you would be admitted to a chemical dependency center for a seven- to ten-day evaluation."

"You gotta be kidding."

"Nope, and there's more. The contract calls for no privileges the first two weeks. No phone calls, in or out; no evenings out; no extracurricular activities. Nothing except school. Then privileges can be earned after you show responsible behavior, which involves no shouting at people; no name calling; no swearing; no hitting, throwing, or breaking things. Responsible behavior also means doing whatever household chores are assigned and keeping yourself, your room, and your belongings clean and tidy. It also means attending all school classes and completing all assigned homework. Then, after following the contract for two weeks, privileges are earned. If the rules are broken, privileges are removed, as determined by you and your parents in advance. Which privileges are lost and for how long will depend upon which rules are broken. If you break rules repeatedly for two weeks in a row, then you will be demonstrating that you need a more controlled environment and you'll have to be admitted to a residential setting for a more thorough evaluation."

"I don't believe what I'm hearing."

"There's more. You need to find out what your drinking is all about, so you will be required to see an alcohol/drug counselor at least once a week, and you will need to attend classes on chemical dependency. If these classes are not offered in your school or community, you'll need to attend at least one AA Beginner's meeting each week. I guess that's about it. How does it sound?"

"It sucks, that's how it sounds. You think I'm going to agree to something like that?"

"I don't know. I'm just tossing it out as one possible option. The other is admission to a seven- to ten-day residential chemical dependency treatment center for further evaluation."

"I don't believe this. You gotta be kidding."

"No, I'm not kidding. I'm taking your alcohol involvement very seriously, Allison, and I'm suggesting that you do the same. Go out now into the waiting room and think over these two options while I report my findings and discuss these options with your parents. Then we'll all meet again."

Whenever possible, I like to give kids a choice. Choices help them save face and often gain their willingness to cooperate. I'm usually not concerned about whether they like the choices.

Phyllis and Stuart were not at all surprised that I thought Allison's involvement with alcohol was serious, but they were startled to hear she might be addicted and that I was recommending only two options—the contract as I described it to Allison or immediate admission to the treatment center for evaluation.

At first, both parents wanted a less comprehensive alternative. Stuart wondered why they couldn't use only part of the contract, like getting Allison to agree to see a chemical dependency counselor. Phyllis pointed out that Allison had refused therapy in the past, and that there was little hope of her following through with it this time.

I pointed out that the primary reason they could not achieve success by going at this in a piecemeal fashion was that they had lost a lot of parental power. "Allison follows some of your rules some of the time. But look at the past two years: I think you'll see that Allison has been doing pretty much what she wants, not what you want." Both agreed with me.

"It's essential," I went on, "that you regain control of your own household. The only way that I know of is by starting out with virtually total control of Allison's environment. If she agrees to this contract, and does well with it, the control can be lessened gradually until she demonstrates that she has regained her own control. Right now she's demonstrating a lack of control to some degree, in terms of both yours and her own standards.

"To turn her life around, she has got to stop drinking. Even if she's willing to cooperate, I'm not sure she'll be able to do that within the controlled environment called for in the contract. But I do know that without a controlled environment, either at home or in a treatment center, her chances of stopping are slim.''

I then pointed out that both options addressed Allison's chemical involvement. ''If she's at home, she'll attend special chemical dependency information classes in her school, or AA Beginner's meetings. In addition, she'll be in counseling with someone who can help her understand herself better and teach her about living without mood-altering chemicals. If she goes to an in-patient treatment center, in addition to the evaluation she'll receive, she will learn an enormous amount of information about chemicals and her relationship to them. Either way, I think both Allison and you may very well discover that she is addicted. If so, both options, in turn, will lead her to further treatment. If she's at home, for example, she can increase her AA attendance and get into a professional recovery support group in addition to her individual counseling. If she's in an evaluation center, she will either be referred back home for this kind of therapy package or to a residential chemical dependency treatment center, whichever her degree of involvement warrants. She will not have the choice of an out-patient comprehensive treatment center, since none exists near your home.''

''What if she's not addicted?'' Stuart asked.

''Then she'll just follow the contract, and you can modify it to include fewer rules and more privileges as she demonstrates increased personal control,'' I answered. ''After three months she can stop attending the chemical dependency information meetings in her school or in AA. And in time she can stop her individual therapy. But throughout her adolescent years, I strongly advise that you insist on the no-alcohol-or-other-drug-use part of the contract.''

''Well, what do you think, Phyl?'' Stuart asked. ''Both of these options seem like an enormous undertaking to me, much bigger than I figured on. You know, I still can't get over the fact that she's barely fourteen. She just had her birthday a month ago. Is it really this bad? I've got this fear that we're making it worse than it actually is.''

''When you talk like that, Stu,'' Phyllis said, ''I feel like I'm the only one seeing the problem. Look at all the things we've told Ruth about Allison. Were we making that up? Look at Ruth's evaluation, for God's sake! She's not telling us there's no problem, she's telling us it's even worse than we thought. Stuart, sweetheart, please get with it! I need you desperately. Allison needs you. We both need you.''

''I know, honey. I'm with you, I really am. I'm just scared, scared for our little girl,'' he admitted tearfully, taking Phyllis's hand.

Both wept. Both were facing what no parent ever wants to face. I encouraged them to get help. Both agreed to attend Families Anonymous meetings and to continue in counseling.

Then we discussed Allison's two options in depth. Both shuddered at the very thought of enforcing the contract. I reminded them that the contract was not even an option unless Allison was prepared up front to cooperate fully. ''Then, if at any time she breaks the contract, you will take her to the evaluation center. But I appreciate your concerns. Even with her agreement, you'll have to monitor her behavior and impose the consequences as needed. Families Anonymous meetings and counseling will help, but still the contract is not an easy form of parenting. Frankly, though, I think you'll find it a whole lot easier than the parenting you've been doing without her cooperation.''

Phyllis and Stuart spoke of their fears of having Allison in an evaluation center they knew nothing about. Her only experience away from home, other than overnights at friends' houses or visits to her grandmother, had been the sleep-away camp from which she'd been expelled. Phyllis had heard ''ghastly stories about what happens to kids in drug places.''

I assured them that adolescent chemical dependency centers do not use scare tactics, bullying, or shame-inducing devices. But knowing full well that I, too, would never send a child of mine off to a place I had not investigated, I suggested visiting the center or calling to find out everything they wished to know. I also offered to give them the names and numbers of parents whose children had gone to a chemical dependency center and who were willing to help others face what they had faced.

"What do you think we should do?" Stuart asked. I told them that only they could decide which option was best for them. I suggested that each of them, Allison included, take a week to digest everything we had discussed. In the meantime, I asked Phyllis and Stuart to draw up a contract, including the basic principles I outlined, in case that was the route they chose to take.

Phyllis called before our next appointment. She was working on the contract and wondered if she could put in a clause stating that Allison could not associate with her older, "troubled" friends. I told her that I thought she was going to have enough to handle as it was. Besides, "troubled" friends would lose interest in anyone who followed what they would consider an onerously restrictive contract—although nontroubled peers ordinarily were living within most of its limits. Therefore, the contract itself would govern Allison's friendships. In essence, following it would mean losing "troubled" peers while gaining access to healthy friends.

At our appointment the following week, Phyllis and Stuart told Allison how much they loved her and how scared they were for her. They said they were willing to support her in either choice. Allison said that she didn't like the choices, didn't think they were necessary, and didn't want to pick either. When her parents did not back down, she asked to see the contract Phyllis had drawn up.

CONTRACT

I agree not to use alcohol or other drugs. If I do use alcohol or other drugs, or if my parents or other adults report any alcohol/drug–related behavior of mine such as seeing me use, slurring my words, staggering, paraphernalia, alcohol odor on my breath, or passing out, I agree to enter a residential chemical dependency treatment center for an evaluation.

To earn privileges, I agree to the following seven rules:

1. I agree not to swear, shout at, or call people names; hit; or throw things at people.
2. I agree to daily: bathe, make my bed, keep my clothes and room clean and tidy.
3. I agree to do my assigned chores daily: dinner dishes, table setting, or garbage.
4. I agree to attend all my school classes.
5. I agree to complete all homework as assigned.
6. I agree to attend at least one AA Beginner's meeting each week. [No chemical dependency information classes were held in her school or community.]
7. I agree to see [selected therapist] at least once a week.

By following the above seven rules for two weeks, I will earn the privileges of using the phone, playing in after-school team sports, and going out on Friday and Saturday evenings. I agree not to use the phone after nine at night. I agree to be home by eleven on Friday and Saturday evenings. I agree to come directly home after the games during the week.

I agree that the consequences for not following these seven rules will be suspension of my privileges. Specifically, if I swear, or shout at, or call other people names, or if I do not do my assigned chores, or if I do not keep myself, my room, and my belongings clean and tidy, I agree I will lose phone privileges two days for each infraction. Specifically, if I hit people or throw or break things in anger, or if I skip any school classes, or if I do not do my homework as assigned, or if I do not keep my curfews, or if I skip either my therapy session or my AA meeting, I agree I will lose permission to go out on one weekend evening for each infraction. If I lose permission to go out on both Friday and Saturday nights two weeks running, I agree I will be admitted to a residential chemical dependency treatment center for further evaluation.

Allison said that she would agree to the contract, but she wanted some parts of it changed. She didn't want to wait two weeks for privileges. She also wanted to hang around with friends after school on the days she didn't have games, and insisted her parents had no right to keep her from doing these things.

Phyllis and Stuart stood firm. They said that she could have the privileges listed on the contract, but only after she had earned them. Allison then said she would earn her privileges, but she wouldn't go to AA. Phyllis and Stuart said attendance at AA was not negotiable. Then Allison objected to the consequences. She thought she should lose phone privileges for only one night, not two, which Phyllis and Stuart granted. Finally, Allison agreed to follow the contract exactly as written, the one change being the reduction in the suspension of phone privileges.

Fortunately, Allison had two things going for her—things that enabled her to finally agree to the contract, despite her initial protests. First, her parents had provided a structured environment throughout her childhood so that she had internalized discipline, some of which she still retained despite her harmful alcohol involvement. Second, Allison's chemical abuse had not progressed to the point of totally destroying the values

155

her parents had helped instill. Here was an adolescent who, deep down, still wanted to please her parents, who wanted to be loved by them, and who wanted to succeed at her life.

As a result of our hard work together, Phyllis, Stuart, and Allison now had reasonable, agreed-upon rules, enforceable consequences for noncooperation; and an educational/treatment component to help Allison stay on track. For the first time, Phyllis and Stuart were in a position to let go and allow Allison to take care of herself, or fail. Prepared for either eventuality, they could now start concentrating on taking care of themselves.

Written contracts are especially helpful for children like Allison, who have a history of breaking family rules and standards of behavior. Other children, like Mark, who have not presented as many disciplinary problems at home, do not require written contracts. They need only a clearly stated rule requiring no alcohol or other drug use, a workable treatment plan, and more intensive treatment as a consequence for breaking the no-chemical-use rule.

Inside addiction, there is a pained person trying to get out. Usually he or she is armored with so much defensiveness—hostility, blaming, lying, denying, and rationalizing—that about all we can see is the armor. Probably because of all the consequences he was facing as a result of his chemical use, Mark's defensive armor was falling apart. Thus the hidden, pained person was revealed at our first session.

As with other addicted persons, Mark's chemical use went against everything he valued: his relationship with his dad, his own high standards of performance, his love of adventure and nature, and his own hopes for his future. Mark had been warring with himself for just about the entire time he had been using chemicals.

As addiction progresses and chemicals gain an ever-increasing hold, a person finds that his values eventually give way. One characteristic of late-stage addiction is that the conflict between values and behavior virtually ceases. At this point, addicted young persons may commit all kinds of deviant acts, from prostitution to armed robbery, seemingly without conscience. The values are still there, of course, but addiction completely suppresses them.

Fortunately, Mark's addiction had not progressed that far. While he claimed that being expelled from school did not matter, he knew it really did, and so did the pain he knew he was causing his father. Once he'd aimed for his dad's alma mater, Princeton, but now he was not too sure he'd be accepted. That mattered. And it also worried him that he'd lost control over his chemical use. "I've spent so much of my life facing and conquering challenges," he admitted. "It's just too much knowing I've been bulldozed by booze and dope. I climb mountains and then get defeated by drugs. Christ! Help me get out of this! What can I do?"

Since Mark was readily admitting to his problem and wanting help so badly, he seemed an excellent candidate for outpatient treatment. While he claimed he had never suffered any withdrawal symptoms, Mark had not gone without chemicals long enough for either of us to be certain he was not physically addicted as well. So we agreed on an out-patient treatment package with the understanding that medical care would be provided should withdrawal symptoms occur.

Mark's school was willing to readmit him as long as he was in therapy and in active recovery, and it offered a chemical dependency recovery support group every Thursday afternoon. With his father's approval, Mark agreed to the following treatment plan: he would stop using all drugs including alcohol, attend the school's weekly recovery support group, enter individual counseling with a professional experienced in

157

addiction, and attend at least three AA meetings each week. Bill and Mark both agreed that if Mark was not able to stop using, he would be admitted to a residential chemical dependency treatment center. Mark also agreed to continue following other household rules regarding school attendance, completion of homework, assigned chores, personal hygiene, respectful behavior, and curfews.

I recommended that Bill attend Al-Anon or Families Anonymous meetings on a regular weekly basis for help in handling the pain associated with Mark's addiction. Bill was quite sure that most of his pain would diminish now that Mark was addressing his problem. I reminded him that things might not work out quite so neatly, and that the self-help groups would always be available.

Putting together a viable treatment plan for someone like Mark, who is in control of much of his behavior, admits to a problem, and wants help, is easy. Self-help groups are readily available and can form the basis of the treatment plan. Putting together a plan for someone like David, who is in control of his behavior but who denies a chemical problem and does not want help, is not so simple, especially when extensive chemical use is suspected but undocumented.

As you will recall, the first time I saw David he was markedly arrogant. His mother, Karen, had perceived no behavior/personality changes, however, and had no evidence of chemical use other than his "one shot" at cocaine and occasional beer drinking. David said that he had tried marijuana but didn't like it. He admitted to trying cocaine once, said he didn't like the effects of hard liquor, and only occasionally drank beer. He made a promise not to use alcohol or other drugs in the future.

A few weeks later, Karen brought David back to see me because she had found the beer cans, rolling papers, and a cellophane packet coated with white powder. At this appointment David was overtly hostile, denying any association with the paraphernalia his mother had discovered, to the point where he denied that it was drug paraphernalia.

David's father was told by school officials that David was disrespectful of assignment rules, had cut classes, and had forged excuses. He was also told that David's best friend had recently been expelled for using cocaine.

We had some smoke here, but did we have a fire? I was almost certain that David's involvement with chemicals was far more extensive than he reported. For one thing, too much drug paraphernalia had been found subsequent to a promise of no chemical use. Also, repeated cocaine use usually indicates a prior heavy involvement with alcohol and/or marijuana. Third, if his best friend was a coke user, it was highly likely that David was, too. I told all of this to David and his parents, but I also said that I had to agree with David that we did not have enough evidence to ''convict'' him.

At home David was following his mother's rules, and showing only a few signs of chemical use and behavior/personality changes. Most chemical dependency treatment centers would be reluctant to admit David for an evaluation with such limited data. David, locked into denial, would feel out of place at AA Beginner's meetings and would lose respect for his parents' credibility for sending him to AA on such limited evidence.

With David and other adolescents who are following household rules and showing only a few recent signs of chemical use and behavior/personality changes, I encourage parents to back off. Let time tell. Give the child the space and support to prove he's okay, try for more positive parent/child interactions, and create more shared activities. I also ask parents to secure a promise from their child not to use any chemicals, with the understanding that the consequences for breaking the promise twill then be a treatment plan similar to Allison's or admission to a residential chemical dependency center for further evaluation and possible treatment. I also offer referrals for family or individual therapy with professionals knowledgeable about chemical dependency. The parents and the child should attend classes on chemical dependency if such sessions are locally available.

Since David was following the household rules, he did not need a written contract. But he did need a clearly stated rule regarding no alcohol or other drug use, and a meaningful consequence for breaking that rule. David's parents, Karen and Cliff, felt that a consequence involving attendance at AA Beginner's meetings and individual counseling would prove too lengthy, as David was nearing the end of high school and preparing for college. Therefore, they opted for the shorter-term residential evaluation, allowing whatever treatment was warranted to be implemented before David left for college.

I encouraged Karen and Cliff to tell David how much they loved him, to share their concerns about his chemical use, to state clearly the no-alcohol-or-other-drug-use rule, and to back off after securing his agreement. They agreed they would all attend classes on chemical dependency offered at a local affiliate of the National Council on Alcoholism, and turned down the offer of individual or family therapy. Both Karen and Cliff agreed to attend Families Anonymous meetings.

"Dave, we've decided to go with you on this one," his father said, as the four of us met in my office to go over the terms of the unwritten contract. Immaculately dressed in his customary prep school garb, David still appeared to be Mr. Cool. But I detected a thin crack in his Ivy League armor: three unwavering adults were obviously in agreement about a plan of action. "There's not enough evidence to convict you," Cliff continued, "and besides, that's the last thing we want to do. I love you, Dave, very much, and so does your mother.

But we don't like the changes in you, and we're worried about how alcohol and drugs can hurt you. So, what we've decided is no more class cuts, no more forging, and no more disrespect toward teachers. Are you in agreement so far?''

"Yes," David replied, looking relieved. No doubt he had expected much worse.

"And it means no more alcohol," Karen went on, "and that includes beer. No more drinking at all until you're of legal age. And no drugs of any kind. David, I love you very, very much. I don't want to lose you. Will you agree not to drink alcohol or use any other drugs?''

"Yes. I promise you I won't drink alcohol or use drugs."

"You've already made that promise once, Dave," his father reminded him. "And I want you to know that I consider the paraphernalia your mother found to be evidence that you broke it. This time, if you do drink or use other drugs, or if we see any signs of use, we're going to assume you're hooked. Do you understand? There are no extenuating circumstances here. No acceptable reasons for breaking your agreement. Drinking even one beer, doing any kind of drugs at all, having any paraphernalia is going to tell us you're into something bigger than you can handle by yourself. You'll have to be admitted to a residential chemical dependency center for an evaluation and possible treatment. Are you clear on this?''

"Yes."

"Do you agree not to use, and to go to the chemical dependency center if you do use?''

"Yes."

"Good. Do what you say you're going to do, and we'll back off. Then we can all get on with our lives. Oh, one last thing. Your mother and I are going to attend a series of classes on addiction and we expect you to go with us. Okay?''

"Okay."

"So, who's hungry? We've said our piece, Karen, so let's

go eat. How about you, Dave? You look like you could go for a burger and some fries.''

With adolescents like David, who follow household rules and show few signs of chemical use and behavior/personality changes, parents have much to gain by stating the rules and consequences regarding chemical use and then backing off. It allows the child to prove himself. If the child then uses chemicals, he is demonstrating to himself as well as to others that he is in need of further evaluation and perhaps treatment, which can then be obtained as agreed.

Three weeks after he made his agreement not to use alcohol or other drugs, David arrived home two hours past his curfew—staggering, slurring his words, obviously drunk. The next day he was on a plane, on his way to a chemical dependency center, where he was found to be addicted.

David had hidden his addiction well. His evaluation at the center revealed that he had been using marijuana daily for several years, alcohol several times a week for several years, and cocaine two or three times a week for close to a year. David says he became willing to reveal his chemical history once he broke the agreement. "I wasn't convinced I had a problem when I made the promise, but I wanted to keep it. I knew it was fair, and I also wanted to show my parents that I really appreciated how well they were working together on this. They're divorced and their joint support meant a lot to me. I wanted to keep up my end of the bargain. But I couldn't. Then I knew I needed help."

In summary, parents can be guided toward a determination of the extent of their child's harmful involvement by looking at the child's degree of denial, unwillingness to cooperate, loss of control over behavior, and extensiveness of chemical use, including duration, amount, frequency, and type of chemical.

The greater the degree of these factors, the more harmful the involvement.

Those adolescents moderately involved—those who are somewhat similar to Allison, Mark, or David—are candidates for out-patient care, so long as they agree to a contract, written or not, that includes a no-chemical-use rule and a consequence for breaking the rule, such as more extensive treatment or a more controlled environment. Such a possibility should always be part of the contract. In addition, the contract should include rules of behavior, along with the consequences for not abiding by them.

In the next chapter we will discuss those teenagers heavily involved—like Ricky, Brad, JoAnn, and Tim—who are candidates for residential care. These adolescents are treatable, but they do require highly controlled treatment environments. And most will require specially designed efforts on their parents' part to get them to agree to enter, and cooperate with, residential treatment.

For a more definitive determination of a child's chemical involvement and consequent needs, parents should seek professional advice. Chemical dependency is a *disease*. It needs to be *diagnosed*. If it exists, it needs to be *treated*. Parents normally do not diagnose or prescribe treatment or rely upon home remedies for other diseases. What they usually do is seek help from those professionals specially educated and trained in the diagnosis and treatment of the disease. *Chemical dependency should be approached in the same way.*

TWELVE

How to Help Kids Who Are Unwilling to Cooperate: The Structured Intervention

Do any of us ever really want treatment? Does a woman with a cancerous breast want a mastectomy? Does anyone want root canal work? No, of course not. We seek treatment out of need, not want. It would seem that persons suffering from chemical dependency and codependency should also seek treatment out of need. Yet because both child and parents have an illness they cannot see, they often do not recognize their need.

As we have said, chemically dependent adolescents are shrouded in a blanket of denial that tells them they are well when in fact they are ill. Often, the more advanced their addiction, the stronger their denial and the greater their reluctance to seek treatment.

A father in one of my therapy groups recently joked, "I was so codependent that if I'd died, my daughter's life would have passed before my eyes." So true. Codependents can become so focused on others that they can barely see themselves, much less their own illness. As with chemical dependency, the more advanced the codependency, the stronger the denial, and the greater the reluctance to seek treatment.

We have all heard the statement "You can't help an alcoholic until he wants help.'' *It's not true. And it's dangerous.* Alcoholics, and persons addicted to other drugs, *can be helped even when they do not want help.* If left to their own devices, most will go to the grave before they seek treatment.

I worked for many years in a residential chemical dependency treatment center where the doors were unlocked and the patients voluntarily admitted. Yet most were there only because they were forced. Their families had said, ''Treatment or no home''; bosses had said ''Treatment or no job''; judges had said, ''Treatment or jail''; or they were so sick it was clearly ''Treatment or death.'' They were in treatment because they were *forced* to be—and most of them got well.

Because it is highly structured and carefully designed with both educational and treatment components in mind, residential chemical dependency treatment is highly motivational. It is designed to help chemically dependent persons *see* their illness. Classes are given, movies are shown, stories are told, and reading materials are assigned. Chemically dependent patients are given more information about their illness than doctors, nurses, social workers, and psychologists receive in professional school. And therapy groups and individual counseling enable patients to gain insight into their defenses and express their underlying feelings. Once patients perceive their illness, they become motivated for personal change. Then the treatment is designed to help chemically dependent adolescents put their lives together in ways that work.

Codependent parents are treated in a similar manner during family week at the treatment center. Most parents enter treatment out of a desire to help their child, but through it they learn about their own illness and receive therapy designed to help them improve their own lives.

Teenagers and young adults with an extensive chemical involvement who have repeatedly shown several behavior/personality changes, or who have not been able to follow an out-patient treatment plan, or who are uncontrollable at home should receive treatment in a residential setting. What happens if they refuse? Their parents should then seek special intervention counseling that offers treatment in a manner few chemically dependent children refuse. (Usually intervention counseling can be provided by the addiction specialist who has helped determine the child's treatment needs. If not, the specialist can usually recommend someone trained in interventions. Or parents can call the local affiliate of the National Council on Alcoholism, out-patient chemical dependency agencies, hospitals with chemical dependency units, and chemical dependency treatment centers, which either provide, or know of, private practitioners who provide such counseling. All are listed in local telephone directories.)

Interventions are highly choreographed. A prepared team of concerned persons—parents, siblings, other relatives, non-addicted friends, and/or other concerned persons—meet with the chemically dependent child, usually in the intervention counselor's office. During the meeting they present the child with data regarding his chemical use and related behavior, with the intention of expressing love and concern and offering treatment. If at the end of the team presentation the child refuses treatment, he is then informed that the consequence of refusal is losing the right to live at home.

Interventions work, in some cases because treatment is less onerous than its alternative. Yet interventions often work before the child even hears of the alternative.

Why? Most, if not all, addicted persons actually want out; they just don't know how to get out. Asking for help—in the face of their denial which asserts that they are well and that others, particularly parents, are crazy—represents an enormous loss of face. With a structured intervention, chemically dependent adolescents can save face. They can accept treatment because they have been "forced into it," or because they have "no choice," not because they are admitting to a need. They can hang on to their denial all the way to the treatment center.

But interventions work for another reason as well. Addiction is incredibly degrading. Addicts no longer value themselves. Yet a structured intervention is a loving process. Although the child hears data about chemical use and related behavior, he still comes away with the feeling that he is loved. Many adolescents agree to treatment for the very simple reason that the intervention has made them, for the first time, feel worthy of treatment.

When considering a structured intervention, most parents look at the odds: nationwide, over 90 percent of chemically dependent adolescents select the parent's choice of treatment. Under 10 percent choose the street or a court-appointed center. Some parents automatically believe they will lose; they are so used to not having anything work with their child, they assume nothing will work. But although chemically dependent kids may be crazy, they are not insane. They know which side of the bread the butter is on. And if they can't see the butter right away, most do once they hit the streets.

In my private practice only one young person has refused his parents' treatment offer after an intervention. Most of us even expected he might refuse since he knew that if his parents no longer let him live at home, he could live with his addicted girlfriend. Two months later, while living with his girlfriend, he had his jaw broken in a bar fight. He called to ask his parents if their treatment offer still held. Of course it did.

Chemical dependency is progressive and fatal unless treated. Parents who do not take measures to insist upon treatment become part of the illness. Each passing day further threatens the child. Many, like Ricky, die right in their parents' home. Others are killed in traffic accidents, bar fights, or drug deals gone wrong. Or they get AIDS. Or they pass out and drown in their own vomit. Or they overdose or commit suicide. *It is extremely dangerous to enable this sickness.*

Yet parents are terrified of backing out of their enabling roles, of forcing the issue of treatment. Although their child faces death every day right before their eyes, many codependent parents are convinced that their child will commit suicide or be killed if he is given an ultimatum.

Part of this fear comes from their own codependency. They have become so dependent upon their child that they project this dependence, assuming he needs them as much as they need him. Nothing could be further from the truth. Addiction causes gross distortions in the child's perceptions of his needs. While actively addicted, only two things matter to an adolescent: using chemicals and having an environment conducive to use.

A large part of the parents' fear is, of course, based on reality. Court-appointed settings often do not offer quality care, and the streets are dangerous. What parents need to recognize is that their homes are equally dangerous—perhaps even more so, since their homes provide the environment addicted children depend upon in order to continue using.

The fear expressed most frequently by parents as they contemplate a structured intervention is that their child will commit suicide. *Recognize that the structured intervention offers hope*, a light at the end of the addiction tunnel. Enabling offers no hope. Without hope, addicted children are at a very high risk of suicide.

Most parents offer their child treatment over and over and over, only to find that their offer means nothing. *As long as parents remain trapped in their enabling posture, their offers of treatment are truly meaningless.* Such offers do not spell hope for the simple reason that the child realizes his parents are committed to providing an environment conducive to chemical use.

Treatment offered in a professional setting by a group of

prepared, united, loving people, including parents whose tack has clearly changed, is a totally different matter. Far more often than not, the child sees the light and accepts the offered treatment. But intervention is a process, not an event. Therefore, even if the child chooses the street, or a court-appointed setting, the parents' offer of treatment still holds. The light still shines at the end of the tunnel. And, as long as the child has that light, no matter where he is, the chances for suicide are reduced. The chance that the chid will accept treatment still exists.

Recall Mary and Marty. What hope did Tim have in the face of their enabling? They offered treatment repeatedly, begging or threatening, but they did not insist. Day after day, year after year, they provided Tim with an environment conducive to continued chemical use. Their words, urging treatment, meant nothing; their actions, supporting chemical use, meant everything.

Despite the advanced nature of Mary's and Marty's codependency, I thought it highly likely that preparing for a structured intervention would help them to begin to move out of their enabling posture. In turn, despite the intensity of Tim's addiction, I believed that the intervention would motivate Tim to enter a residential chemical dependency treatment center.

In the meantime, because of Tim's recent paranoia and increased violence, Mary and Marty had to learn immediately how to protect themselves. After discussing their fears of involving Tim in the legal system, Mary and Marty agreed to seek a temporary order of protection from the family court the next day, and to call the police if Tim should become violent. Jenny, their youngest daughter, promised, "If they don't, you can be sure I will."

I then told them about the structured intervention process. Highly skeptical that an intervention would work with Tim, they were nevertheless willing to learn more about the process. They scheduled biweekly sessions with me, arranged to attend a series of classes on chemical dependency given at the local affiliate of the National Council on Alcoholism, and agreed to start attending Al-Anon.

They asked Gene, their oldest son, and his wife, Annemarie, to attend the classes with them, since both would be needed at the intervention. Both agreed. Jenny was also no problem. "I've been trying to get my parents to do something for years; of course I'll go." Peggy, their oldest daughter, and her husband, Jim, lived in another state, but Mary and Marty thought they would agree to be part of the intervention. In lieu of the classes, they were asked to read any one of several books explaining the intervention process. (See the bibliography section at the end of this book.) Jenny also asked Paul, one of Tim's former friends who had previously expressed his concern, to attend the classes and participate in the intervention.

Since Tim had progressed about as far as one can go into addiction, residential treatment was a necessity. The more advanced the illness, the more comprehensive the treatment must be.

Mary, with clear foresight, had secured basic and major medical insurance coverage for Tim two years previously, which meant he could receive treatment at any of the many excellent in-patient chemical dependency treatment centers in the United States.

Things were looking up. I could sense that Mary, Marty, and Jenny were feeling a spark of hope. I told them that I believed they could turn everything around and get Tim to agree to accept treatment. Then he would have a good chance of getting well.

Over the next several weeks, each member of the intervention team—Mary, Marty, Jenny, Gene, Annemarie, Peggy,

Jim, and Paul—drew up a list of incidents related to Tim's chemical use and behavior over the past several years. Needless to say, most of them had rather lengthy lists.

Mary balked a couple of times along the way, wanting to stop the whole process. She decided that Tim had a self-esteem problem and that we were going at it the wrong way. She thought that if he got treatment for his self-esteem, he would stop using chemicals and everything would be okay. Gradually she was able to see that his chemical use was probably the cause of his lowered self-esteem, and that in any case the chemical use had to be treated before anything else could be addressed.

One evening Tim became violent, throwing dishes off the table because Marty said something he didn't like. But Marty and Mary did not call the police. "Listen, you don't have any control in your household," I pointed out, "and Tim needs to be controlled. It's very dangerous there, for all of you. You need the law behind you. Only the police can provide the control you and Tim need right now. Besides, if you call the police, Tim will know you're changing, and he needs to see some changes so you'll be more credible at the intervention." When they continued to express reluctance, I told them that I would not work with them any longer if they were not willing to call the police in the face of Tim's violence.

They called the police the next evening. Tim had banged down the door to Jenny's room; he thought that FBI agents were in there "doing things." The next morning, Tim was brought home from the police station. He has been calm since.

Meanwhile, Mary and Marty told Tim that they were attending classes on alcohol and drug problems and were seeing a counselor, who wanted to see him in two weeks. At first he said that he would not see the counselor, but then said he might. They gave him the date, which in fact was the date of the intervention itself, but at no time told Tim anything about the intervention process or that others were involved. But they did, once again, ask Tim if he wanted help. As we had agreed, they told him about the in-patient chemical dependency treatment center near their home and asked if he would be willing to go there, in the hope that they could avoid the structured intervention. Tim refused.

Mary made arrangements for Tim's admission to the chemical dependency treatment center on the afternoon of the scheduled intervention. Without Tim's knowledge, she packed a bag with his clothes and toilet articles.

The team then assembled for the rehearsal of the intervention, which went quite well. Every member of the team had a list of specific chemical-related incidents, and their feelings about those incidents. They learned how to present their data and set the order of presentation. They also discussed their feelings about the intervention—how going behind Tim's back didn't seem right; how they were sure he'd never forgive them, yet how loving and gentle the process now seemed; how they could see that nothing else would work, and how the intervention might succeed. We were left with two items of unfinished business: the consequences of Tim's refusing treatment and the mechanics of getting him to the intervention the next morning.

At various times prior to the rehearsal, Mary, Marty, and I had discussed parental enabling and its danger for everyone. We had agreed that if Tim were allowed to go on like this, he would surely die. Our discussions were reinforced by the information they were receiving at the chemical dependency information classes. I also had asked Mary and Marty to consider what they might do if Tim refused to accept treatment at the end of the intervention, so this question was not new to them.

At the rehearsal, we thoroughly reviewed exactly what Tim's refusal would mean to everyone on the team. How would it make them feel? What actions were they prepared to take? Could Tim continue to live at home? Mary and Marty both agreed that if Tim refused treatment, he was out—on his own. They knew they would feel devastated, but that they were fully prepared to leave him and his suitcase in the parking lot next to my office.

"Do you really mean that?" I asked.

They both said yes. They said they could see that staying home, staying addicted, would totally destroy Tim and them. Yes, they were ready to offer him the choice of either seeking treatment or leaving their home. All the members of the team supported Mary and Marty in their decision.

"He may put you to the test tomorrow," I pointed out. "Are you going to be able to actually leave him in the parking lot? Think about that. Can you really do that?"

Both wept—long, deep, gut-wrenching sobs. "Oh God! I'm so scared," Mary cried. "What will he do? What if it rains? Where will he go?"

"That's his problem, Mom," Gene said, softly. "You're offering him treatment. If he doesn't want that, he should be kicked out of the house."

Annemarie asked about other addicted kids in this situation. "What happens? Do they get kicked out?"

"They certainly lose the right to live at home," I told her frankly. "Once they see that their parents are serious, most opt for treatment, but you can't depend on that. That's why I want you all fully prepared for the worst tomorrow."

"What about minors?" Paul wondered. "Do they get put out of the house?"

"Yes," I answered, "but in a different way. We encourage parents to work with the courts. Then the kids are given a choice—either the treatment their parents offer or the treatment the court offers."

"We've got to do it, Mary," Marty urged. "And I can't do it alone. We need to be together on this."

"I know it needs to be done, but I don't know if I can handle it," Mary replied.

"We'll help you handle it, Mom," Jenny offered. "Peggy and Jim are staying with us over the weekend. Dad and I'll be with you, and Gene and Annemarie can come over. We'll all help you, Mom." After more discussion, Mary decided that she would be able to do whatever was needed the next day.

Each of the other team members then spoke of what a refusal would mean to them. They each had reached a point of not wanting to have anything to do with Tim if he refused treatment and said they were prepared to tell him that.

As far as Mary and Marty knew, Tim was still planning to keep his appointment with me. In fact, the day before, he had asked what time it was scheduled. But if he refused at the last moment, they agreed to tell Tim they were prepared to call the police. He now knew, of course, that they were capable of doing that, since they had already done it. Tim's order of protection stated that Tim could not use alcohol or drugs in the house. Since he was using both, they had every right to call the police, and Tim knew it.

The members of the intervention team settled themselves in my office a half hour before Mary and Marty were due to arrive with Tim. Everyone was nervous. Since sometimes cocaine users are too agitated to sit for any length of time, we had agreed that if Tim seemed on edge, everyone would present only two or three of their chemical-related incidents and their feelings about them. Otherwise, they would present everything on their lists in order to give Tim a fuller picture of his chemical use. Chemically dependent persons cannot see themselves with any degree of accuracy, so they are in need of data from others—and the more, the better.

We had also agreed not to attempt to stop Tim if he did bolt. Instead, Paul would follow him out and attempt to talk him into coming back into the office. At that point, everyone thought Tim would be better able to listen to a friend than a family member.

The team was well prepared but, naturally, apprehensive. No one could be sure what Tim would do, and all wondered how he would react when he spotted all of them sitting in my office. Needless to say, Tim was surprised but acted as if nothing were out of the ordinary—which, in fact, is a typical response at interventions. Tim kissed Annemarie and Peggy, whom he had not seen in several months, ignored Jenny, and shook hands with Gene, Jim, and Paul, whom he had not seen in over a year.

After he sat down, I explained to him that I had asked everyone to come today because they loved him and were concerned about his alcohol and drug use. "They want to talk to you, Tim, about their concerns. Will you listen to them?" He nodded, and I told him he'd have a chance to speak after they had finished.

"Tim," Gene began, "I love you. I'm here today because nothing I've done has helped you in the past, and I want to help you.

"Three years ago, Tim, when you worked for me on the spring cleanups, you had agreed to the terms of employment— that you would not drink or smoke pot. The first month you were terrific. You worked hard and you were a pleasure to have on the job. Then all that changed. I could see then that you were really hooked, and it scared me."

"What's going on here?" Tim interrupted. "I have to listen to this crap?"

"I know this is hard for you, Tim," I reassured him. "Think you can hang in? They're really scared and hurting; they need to talk. Okay?"

"Yeah, yeah, get it over with."

"At Christmas at our house last year you drank so much

175

wine that you passed out and fell off your chair while we were eating," Gene said. "I was scared, Tim, and, frankly, disgusted.

"Jenny called a few months ago, telling me you had tried to strangle Dad. She was crying so hard that she could barely speak. I felt helpless and angry at you for hurting Dad and scaring Jenny like that.

"You were stoned at your high school graduation. Maybe the others couldn't see it, but I could. God, I felt so sad. I was drunk at my graduation, too, and it really hurt to see you following the same path.

"You were drunk at my wedding reception, so drunk I had to get a bunch of guys to haul you out. I was angry that you messed up our day like that.

"Last spring, when you and I were sitting out on the back porch, you told me you were a zombie, a drugged-out zombie. I felt helpless. You don't have to be a zombie, Tim. There's help for you, good help, and I hope you'll take it."

Tim was not wired and ready to bolt as we had feared. He sat quietly, not showing much reaction. He kept his head lowered, not making any eye contact. Neatly dressed and freshly shaven, Tim had obviously taken pains to put on a good appearance today. I was touched. It showed part of the appealing side of Tim that everyone had talked about, the real Tim underneath the addiction.

"Tim, I love you . . . I love you so much," Marty gulped, breaking into the sobs of a father mourning his lost son.

Tim turned to me. "Is this necessary? Let's just skip it and get on to whatever point you're trying to make."

"We can't," I answered. "It's hard, Tim, I know that. Hard for them, hard for you. But this needs to be done. Okay?"

"It's your show," he replied.

After several minutes, Marty was able to continue. "Two

summers ago, up at the lake when we were fishing, I was so happy. You were clean, off the sauce and off the dope. You looked so good, like your old self. It was great spending that week with you like that. But that's the last time, Tim, that you've been clean. I've missed you more than I can say. And I'm scared. I'm afraid you're going to die.

"Four years ago, one of the restaurant owners you worked for came up to me on the street. He said that he felt he owed it to me to tell me why he fired you: because you were a drunk. I felt so ashamed. I didn't know what to say to him.

"These past years have been a nightmare. You smoke pot all day, and at night all you do is argue and pick fights. I can't go on like this any longer. I'm tired, so tired of your addiction.

"Two months ago, your mother found a supply of crack in the pocket of her windbreaker that you had worn. You said you'd been using crack for months, and you laughed. God, I wanted to die; I was so scared for you.

"Three weeks ago, you knocked Jenny's door down because you thought FBI agents were in there. This is it, Tim, the end of the line for us. I hope you'll take the help we're offering today."

Mary was tearful but able to speak. "Tim, I love you with all my heart. And I'm here today because I want to help you.

"Six months ago, I had to go to work with an ugly bruise on my cheek. I told everyone I had fallen. I lied, Tim, because I was ashamed to tell them you had thrown a plate at me when you were drunk.

"At Thanksgiving last fall, when the whole family was together at our house, you spent the entire day in the basement, all by yourself, smoking pot. You wouldn't even join us when we sat down to eat. That's your favorite meal, Tim. You always used to help me make the dressing, remember? I felt sad. I was lonely without you.

"A few months ago, when Aunt Jean was up from Florida

and spent the weekend with us, you got drunk, and when she said something about your drinking, you told her to mind her business. And you called her a stupid old slut. I was hurt and embarrassed.

"One Saturday last winter, when your car was being fixed, you borrowed mine and said you'd pick me up at the mall. I waited and waited, outside where you told me you'd be. You finally showed up, but it was freezing out, Tim, and I got so cold. Then when I got in the car, you were drunk but you insisted on driving. You were speeding and kept veering into the on-coming lane. The traffic was heavy and I thought you were going to kill us. I've never been so scared in my life.

"I don't invite people over anymore because I never know what you're going to be like. I'm lonely, Tim. I miss my friends. I hate what your drinking and drugging is doing to you and to us.

"It was wonderful being with you at the lake when you were not drinking or doing dope. You were fun, so warm and caring, like my old Tim. I want you back. I want my Tim back. I love you, Tim, and I hope with all my heart that you will get help."

"I only see you at holidays, Tim," Jim, Tim's brother-in-law, spoke up. "Only a few times a year, but each time you're always stoned. Your drugging puts a damper on all our holidays, and I resent that.

"Last Christmas, little Jimmy got upset when you fell off your chair. He cried. He thought you were dead. How do I explain to a five-year-old child that his uncle was drunk?

"Peggy's always worried about you. We live 300 miles from here, and your addiction is still interfering with our lives. Peggy even canceled some important plans we had a few weeks ago so she could come home and see if her parents were all right after you'd gone on that rampage and pulled all the phones out of the walls. I really resent your addiction and how it's hurting my family.

"I asked your parents not to bring you to our house for Easter this year because I didn't want my children to be exposed to any more of your drunken behavior. I don't know who you are, Tim. I've never seen you anything but stoned. I hope you will get the help that's being offered here today. I'd like to be able to get to know you."

"Timmy, I'm here because I love you very much," Annemarie began, with tears in her eyes. "When Gene and I first started to date, you were just beginning high school. I always liked you; you were so bright and cheerful and fun to be around. But the alcohol and drugs have changed you.

"A few months ago, at my house, you had been drinking and you started raving, shouting that you were going to kill yourself. I was scared.

"Our first baby will be born in a few weeks, Tim. But we can't even think about asking you to be the godfather, not unless you get help and get well.

"I miss you at the holidays, Tim, when you drink or do dope and stay off by yourself. And I miss you as a brother. Please get help."

"Hey there, old buddy," Paul said. "We've been best friends since nursery school, but I had to stop seeing you because the booze and drugs have turned you mean. I'm here now, Tim, because I still care about you and because I'd like my old friend back. I miss you, Tim. I really do. I hope you'll get help. Oh Christ, Tim," Paul sobbed. "Don't die out on me, man. I want you back. Get help. For crissakes don't die."

I looked over at Tim to see how he was reacting to his friend's plea. Everyone in the room was in tears. Paul had struck a chord in all of us, but not, apparently, in Tim. He sat placidly, looking off at the wall or down at the floor, seemingly unmoved.

After a few moments, his sister Peggy said, "Timmy, I'm here today because I love you very much. I think about you all the time, even though I don't live at home. I love you and I'm scared for you.

"Mom called a couple of months ago. You were stoned, and when she didn't have as much cash on hand as you wanted, you picked up a lamp and threw it at her. God, Tim, how can you do something like that to your own mother? I felt so helpless. Mom calls me a lot, Tim, always with stuff like that to report. And I always feel so helpless.

"You're such a neat brother when you're off the drugs and alcohol. When Sean was born, you drove all the way out to see me and you didn't have drugs in you. We laughed and it was like I had found my kid brother again. I was so incredibly happy. It was like Sean was born and you were reborn. We both talked about how it was a good omen, and that this time you were really going to make it. A week later, Mom said you were using again. Tim, you can make it, I know you can, but not by yourself. You need help."

"I don't know if I'm going to be able to do this, Tim. You make me so damn angry I could kill you. But oh God, Tim," Jenny said tearfully, "I've always loved you so much.

"Remember when we were little? How we did everything together? You used to tell me you would always take care of me. I believed you, Tim. And I need you now. You bitch at me because I'm doing well in school, and you call me 'Miss Clean' 'cause I don't drink or do drugs, but can't you see that I'm still your scared kid sister? Jesus, Tim; I love you so much and need you so much. Will you get help?"

No one said a word. Everyone just sat, wiping their eyes, looking at Tim, waiting for his answer. Jenny asked again, "Tim, will you get help?"

"Yeah, sure I'll get help. I'll take care of it, you don't have to worry," Tim answered.

"The kind of help we're talking about is a chemical dependency treatment center, Tim. Will you agree to that?" Gene asked.

"You gotta be kidding!"

"We're not kidding, Tim. We're not kidding at all. Will you go?" Gene persisted.

"No, I won't go. Is that it?" Tim asked, turning to me. "Do I get my turn to speak now?"

"No, not yet," I answered. "Your refusal to accept the treatment they're offering means something to everyone in this room, including you. You have a right to hear what it means to you."

"Tim, if you refuse the treatment we're offering, you're out," Marty said firmly. "We've got your suitcase packed and in the trunk of the car. You can either go to the treatment center or we're leaving you and your suitcase right here. You're not coming home with us, not today, not ever. Not until you get treatment and get well."

"I can't believe we're really doing this, Tim," Mary added, "but your dad and I are together on this. If you don't go for treatment, you don't come home. We've changed, Tim. Your dad and I aren't going to be part of your addiction any longer, not one day longer." Mary certainly had changed. She spoke firmly and without her usual tears. She sounded very convincing, but I was sure she was dying inside.

Each of the others, in turn, told Tim that they supported his parents' decision and that they did not want to have anything to do with him if he did not agree to seek treatment. Then they got up as rehearsed and prepared to leave.

Tim sat there, stunned. When they were out of the room, he looked at me, his face registering shock, and asked, "What the hell's going on?"

"Your family's leaving."

"What about me? They're just leaving me here like this?"

"Yes."

"Well, what the hell am I supposed to do?"

"I don't know. That's your problem. Do you want a few minutes to reconsider? If so, I'll catch them and ask them to wait."

"Yeah, tell them to wait."

Tim was then given ten minutes to think about his two options—treatment or his loss of the right to live in his parents' home. When it became clear to him that his family had no intention of backing down, he chose to accept treatment.

Tim cooperated throughout his four-week stay at the treatment center, knowing full well that if he did not cooperate, he could not return home. He actually did very well in treatment. However, because of his long history of not functioning, he was referred to a halfway house for six months, where, within the structured environment, he received chemical dependency recovery support therapy as well as assistance in finding and holding a job.

Mary and Marty continued the intervention process following Tim's agreement to enter treatment. Not only did they make it clear they would support nothing but Tim's cooperation with treatment, they continued with their codependency therapy.

Ricky, as you may remember, was also intervened upon with the result that he, too, reluctantly agreed to enter a residential treatment center. But after two weeks Ricky called his parents to say he didn't like treatment. He had several complaints. He was not allowed to smoke in his room, the lounge, or the dining room or during classes and group therapy, which he thought was stupid. He resented having to go to classes on addiction and said he knew more than the counselors. He was responsible for keeping the lounge straightened up and felt such chores were unfair since he was paying to be there. He didn't like his roommate and was annoyed that he couldn't have a room by himself.

After being inundated with such complaints for several days, Ramona and Jim began to waver. I, along with members of their codependent therapy group, pointed out the dangers of supporting Ricky's resistance to treatment and encouraged them to wait at least until after they had attended family week before deciding to let Ricky come home.

But Jim said he had given up. Ramona was crying day and night. Sorry for Ricky, she wanted him home where she thought he would be better off, especially since he was now promising to stay off heroin and to attend Narcotics Anonymous meetings every day. Jim admitted, "I've had it with her. All she does is moan and groan. She wants him home, so let her have him."

Jim acknowledged that he was angry with both Ramona and Ricky and didn't believe for a moment that Ricky would keep his promises. When he saw that giving into Ricky's and Ramona's requests was, in effect, a way of punishing them both, he changed his stance and asked Ramona to wait until they saw Ricky the following week, and Ramona agreed. They both also agreed to increase their number of counseling sessions with me.

But two days later, Ricky called from the airport, demanded a ticket, and came home.

"What could I do?" Ramona asked at her next group therapy session. "I couldn't just leave him stranded at the airport in a strange city."

"Why not?" a member of her group asked. "He could have called the treatment center. They would have taken him back. Or he could have found his own answers. You didn't have to rescue him. Ricky walked out of treatment and you're right back into enabling. You're accepting unacceptable behavior. He's not cooperating, and you're going along with that.''

"Well, he's home, and we're not going to change that now," Jim said. "But Ricky knows he's out if he starts using again. So far he hasn't gone to NA, but he's not using."

A short time later, Ramona and Jim actually did kick Ricky out when he started using heroin and refused to reenter treatment. Soon thereafter they relented, letting Ricky back in the house, where he died of an overdose a few weeks later.

Ramona and Jim seemed to view the intervention as an event rather than the beginning of a process. It was as if they had enough energy to do the structured intervention but not the follow-through. Codependency can be devastating. Not everyone recovers.

If Ramona and Jim had kept their "treatment or no home" offer in effect, in time they would have felt strengthened, and no doubt Ricky would have either stayed in treatment or quickly reentered it. But going back on their word reduced Ricky's chances for recovery. As it turned out, his days were numbered.

Parents do not cause addiction in their children, nor do they knowingly cause codependency in themselves. And although parents are not responsible for their child's recovery, they are responsible for their own recovery.

Sometimes, the recoveries go hand in hand. Failure to recover from chemical dependency can lead to failure to recover from codependency. Likewise, failure to recover from codependency can lead to failure to recover from chemical dependency. On the other hand, recovery from one can lead to recovery from the other.

For example, Brad's parents stayed in codependency therapy and kept their "treatment or no home" offer in effect for years. As a result, they got well, despite Brad's continued illness. And, in time, Brad also started upon his road to recovery.

Barbara and John never did do the actual structured intervention; Brad never gave them that chance. By the time they came to me for help, Brad was eighteen and living in an apartment that they had paid for. "We couldn't stand living with him at home, so we did the next best thing. But he's still caused us all kinds of problems," John reported.

They scheduled the structured intervention twice, and twice Brad promised to come but never showed up. So Barbara and John wrote a letter telling Brad that they loved him and were concerned about his chemical use. They offered him the opportunity to seek treatment at a local chemical dependency center and told him that if he refused, they were no longer going to provide for him.

Brad entered treatment when he was evicted from his apartment and was not allowed back into his parents' home. Then he was kicked out of treatment for lack of cooperation and had to live on the streets. When he broke into his parents' home, they had him arrested. Soon he was back on the streets. After several weeks, Brad got himself readmitted to the treatment center, and this time he followed all the rules. But shortly after his admission to the halfway house—the next step—Brad was caught drinking beer, was expelled, and once again lived on the streets.

And on it went, for close to two years. Then Brad disappeared. Barbara and John didn't hear from him for months. Finally, he called from several states away, saying he was sober and an active member of AA. When he mentioned the possibility of coming home, Barbara and John told him they would first need to have his recovery verified and asked him to have his AA sponsor call them. Brad told them to go to hell. A few days later, he called back to apologize. He said his AA group told him that Barbara and John had every right to want his recovery verified. Brad asked his parents if they would be willing to visit him and meet some of his AA friends as well as his sponsor, which they did. During their visit they also attended Brad's six-month AA anniversary celebration and were impressed by how well he was putting his life back together.

Brad was working as an apprentice carpenter. He lived in an attractive apartment with two other young persons from AA, and went to AA several times a week. He was polite, even charming, and seemed happy. But he said he wasn't sure if he was ready to return home. He knew he eventually wanted to, as well as get his high school equivalency diploma and attend college, yet he felt he needed more time in the recovery support network he had set up for himself.

Barbara and John were relieved. Amazed by Brad's recovery, they were not at all sure they were ready to have him come home. They all agreed that they needed more treatment and more time to prepare for living together under the same roof. So they decided that, if all went well, Brad would return at the end of the summer.

Fortunately, Barbara and John had remained in group therapy for their codependency throughout the turbulent period when Brad was repeatedly in and out of treatment. They also had attended Al-Anon several times a week. Both felt that they never would have been able to hold firm with their "treatment or no home" offer without such support. While saddened and worried about Brad's lack of progress, they were gratified to find themselves getting well despite it. According to Barbara, "At first it was a matter or surviving each day. Gradually it became a matter of wanting to survive, until now we're actually glad to be alive, really glad. Life is good again. We hope and pray life will be good for Brad, too, but we're no longer dependent upon that."

■ ■

JoAnn was deeply moved during her intervention. She cried and hugged her parents, two brothers, three grandparents, one friend, even me—everyone on her intervention team. She said she was so glad to know that everyone still loved her and eagerly accepted their treatment offer.

But in one way her treatment came too late. During the fourth week of her stay in treatment, while Sue Ellen, Matt, and her two brothers were at the center for family week, they learned that JoAnn had tested positive for the AIDS virus. She had no symptoms of the disease, but she did carry the virus.

JoAnn had traded sex for drugs for years. Like Ricky's payment, the price exacted by her addiction is virtually beyond comprehension. But Ricky, had he chosen sobriety, could have lived, while JoAnn, even with sobriety, may not.

THIRTEEN

Kids and Parents in Recovery

One of the first things I did many years ago upon my discharge from a treatment center for chemical dependency was to buy a new nightgown—in preparation for my next hospitalization. I was almost certain that I was not going to be able to stay off alcohol and other drugs. I was an adult with some mature life experiences to fall back on, yet I was still scared. I never did return to chemicals, but it was touch and go for a while.

Many parents assume that once their child is treated, he will quite naturally stay clean and dry, off drugs and alcohol. They minimize the enormous power of the pull toward chemical use, which persists for quite some time. Or they believe that after everything they've done to get their child to treatment, at the very least their child should not return to chemical use. They may even think that after everything their child has suffered as a result of using chemicals, he should know better than to start using again. Or they find it difficult to imagine their child could return to chemicals after a wonderful treatment experience.

Recovery from chemical dependency is an enormous undertaking. Staying off alcohol and other drugs following treatment is not automatic, nor is it natural, easy, or simple. Many teenagers and young adults do make it the first time around. They do stay clean and dry and, slowly but surely, put their lives together in ways that work. But just as many have to be treated again. Some have to be treated again and again and again.

Recovery from chemical dependency developed in adolescence is possible but far more difficult than recovery from chemical dependency developed in adulthood. Teenagers face a peer pressure stronger than any faced by adults. Teenagers and young adults have to work through the painful feelings and difficult tasks of adolescence that adults who develop chemical dependency have already conquered. Many teenagers have to face recovery from a losing posture, so to speak. While they may very well have caught up on some of their schoolwork while in treatment, they may still be behind by several courses, a semester, or a grade once they return to school. In addition, most have the added burden of overcoming a sullied reputation. And they have to leap all these hurdles without the benefit of emotional maturation.

Parents cannot force a child's recovery. They can and should enforce the no-alcohol-or-other-drug-use rule for their child, as well as rules for acceptable behavior. They can and should offer encouragement, praise, and help in exploring options for solving problems. They can and should assume responsibility for their own recovery. And they can and should allow their child to assume responsibility for his own recovery. But they cannot do the actual work of their child's recovery, nor should they try.

In the beginning, chemically dependent adolescents will be excited about their recovery—the new friends they have found, the feelings they have shared, the programs they are in that are so helpful to so many, and the new connections they have made with their families. But the excitement will not last. Soon the realities of their world will encroach on their enthusiasm.

They may feel raw, wounded, vulnerable, full of guilt and shame. They may feel humiliated by the jeers and taunts of their former using-friends. They may feel set apart from the nonusing crowd. They may not know what to do with the free time previously devoted to getting high. They may fear going to parties where beer will be free-flowing and drugs readily available. They may not know how to relate to the opposite sex without chemicals, or how to have fun. They may grow weary of attending self-help meetings several times a week. And like adolescents the world over, they may want out from under parental controls.

Parents may see all of this happening and want to help, but there is really little they can do. *Only the adolescent can face his own world.* Parents can support, praise, encourage, and explore various options with their son or daughter, but they cannot do the coping.

Naturally, parents get anxious when they see their newly recovering chemically dependent child face painful feelings and problems. Rather than discussing their fears and anxieties with each other and members of their support group, many parents attempt to relieve their anxieties by returning to their code-pendent pattern of controlling and fixing. This behavior only breeds increased codependency and creates an environment conducive to chemical use rather than recovery.

Controlling and fixing, as we have seen, take several forms, but two of the most common forms taken by parents in their child's early recovery are the giving of advice and the reducing of demands made upon their child.

Advice sucks, as the kids say. Advice just does not solve problems. It puts the lid on feelings that need to be expressed, and neither resolves painful feelings nor solves problems. Advice makes a kid feel stupid and inadequate, the opposite of how he needs to feel in order to stay clean and dry. Adolescents, chemically dependent adolescents in particular, generally hate advice. Yet many parents coach their child on how to feel and what to do. In essence, they start assuming responsibility for their child's recovery. The more responsibility they claim, the less the adolescent will claim.

Instead of giving advice, parents should encourage their child to explore options. They should pose the question: "How are you going to handle that?" This way they can show respect for the child's ability and judgment. In turn, the child is likely to discuss the matter and to select an option, which the parents can support.

In the face of their recovering child's difficulties and painful feelings, many parents feel that it is cruel or too much of a burden to insist that their child follow the agreed-upon rules. Consequently, when reality sets in, many parents start letting him get away with a messy room, missed curfews, abusive language, or class cuts. By ignoring the agreed-upon consequences, they overlook the rule-breaking behavior, and the child's self-esteem decreases.

Being able to stay clean and dry is dependent in large part upon everyday actions that make one feel good about oneself. Knowing the importance of self-esteem, AA'ers have a saying: "If we want self-esteem, we've got to do esteemable things." Breaking rules is *not* esteemable behavior. Parents do their recovering child a favor when they insist that rules be followed by imposing consequences *whenever* rules are broken.

And if the child breaks the cardinal rule of no alcohol or other drug use, treatment should once again be offered, with the subsequent consequences in the face of its refusal: either court-appointed treatment for a minor, or the loss of the right to live at home if an adult. Under no conditions should parents *ever* overlook a return to chemical use, not one gulp, one drag, one anything. Addiction begins again with the first drink, the first joint, the first snort.

Parents need support—lots of it. I can think of few jobs that are scarier than parenting a child newly recovering from chemical dependency.

In early recovery, trust is nonexistent. Kids don't trust their parents' ability to refrain from codependency any more than parents trust their kids' ability to behave responsibly. Hopes run too high or too low. Fears are enormous and constant. Painful feelings and interactions crop up daily. Old psychic wounds are not yet healed, while new ones are still inflicted. The old codependent parenting model seems incredibly comforting, while letting go is so incredibly frightening. A healthy self-focus seems difficult and unreasonable, while unhealthy child-focus seems easy and appropriate.

Parents need support—self-help groups, codependency counseling, or both—in order to become emotionally healthy and to meet the parental needs of their recovering child. Few parents can work on both tasks without help.

Adolescent chemical dependency is treatable and so is parental codependency. *Recovery is not automatic, natural, easy, or simple, but it is possible.*

How did the young persons in our case histories fare with the help they received? We'll review them in the order we met them.

Both Toni and Brian grew up in communities where teenage alcohol and other drug use was rampant and condoned, and where few, if any, services existed to effectively steer kids away from chemical use.

Both of them faced sets of circumstances virtually designed to lead them toward chemicals. Toni's parents were divorced, and her relationship with her father was estranged and often painful. Her mother worked and was frequently away on business; there were no extended family members available to pick up the slack. Additionally, Toni's formerly close relationship with her mother was deteriorating quickly at the very time she was exposed to a regular chemical use pattern among the peers she was increasingly relying upon.

Brian was handicapped, not only by his learning disability and average IQ in the face of brilliant, high-achieving older brothers, but by his shorter-than-average stature. He also suffered peer rejection.

Looking back upon their adolescence, both Toni and Brian admitted to feelings of isolation and shame—painful feelings, indeed. Neither rated themselves high on the self-esteem ladder. Both, as the saying goes, were accidents about to happen.

Toni had begun to experiment with alcohol and marijuana, but she was not yet a regular chemical user. After breaking her ankle, Toni promised Deborah that she would not drink or use other drugs. Deborah kept close tabs on Toni but saw no further signs of chemical use. So when Toni ran away from home, Deborah sought family therapy. Deborah's action was appropriate for the situation.

Toni got the help she needed to cope with the pain associated with her father, and she, her mother, and her siblings got the help they needed in order to interact with each other in a more nurturing way. As a result of therapy, Toni felt personally empowered to address her circumstances without resorting to chemicals. Another result was that Toni felt emotionally close to her family and had no intention of allowing any alienating factors, like chemicals, to get in the way of that closeness.

Brian's father, Paul, was firm and clear in stating his no-chemical-use rule and the consequences of breaking it. It was clear that his actions were expressions of his love for Brian. Brian was able to stop using chemicals because he was not addicted, and he was willing to stop because he wanted to regain parental approval.

In Toni's case, a parent took action when the first behavior/personality change was evident. In Brian's case, parents took action at the first sign of chemical use.

Today Toni is in graduate school, studying psychology. She does not use drugs but drinks an occasional beer or glass of wine with meals. She does not believe alcohol is an important part of her life, nor does her behavior in any way indicate otherwise.

Brian has been out of college for a year and still is not sure what he wants to do with his life. He is working as a reporter for a small-city newspaper, and he's pondering a career in music. He drinks beer occasionally, has never returned to marijuana, and does not in any way appear to have a harmful chemical involvement.

Ricky is buried out on Long Island. His parents no longer maintain contact with me or the members of their former codependency therapy group.

At no time after agreeing to her contract did Allison show any signs of alcohol or other drug use, and she grudgingly but conscientiously attended her weekly AA meeting and therapy session. However, she repeatedly broke a lot of the other rules in the contract, suffering the agreed-upon consequences. Once, when it appeared she might be grounded both weekend evenings two weeks running, thus facing admission to the residential chemical dependency center, Phyllis suggested that Allison pack her bags and called the treatment center to arrange admission. Overhearing the ensuing telephone conversation, Allison shaped up.

Phyllis and Stuart reported that they would not have been able to follow through on the contract if they hadn't been in Al-Anon and in counseling with an addiction specialist. According to Phyllis, ''It was a drag monitoring her all the time, enduring all her complaints day in and day out. But we were able to hang in with it, and every month Allison became more responsible and cooperative. Without all the help we got, I'm absolutely convinced one or the other of us would have caved in to Allison's incessant complaints and pleas for more freedom. But everyone kept telling us if we gave an inch, Allison would take a yard. So we held firm.''

After three months, Phyllis and Stuart renegotiated the contract. Allison had come to see that she had developed a harmful involvement with alcohol, although she did not believe she had become addicted. Nor did her counselor. Consequently, weekly AA attendance was dropped from her contract and more privileges gradually added as a reward for increasingly responsible behavior.

Nine months after their initial visit, the family came to see me. They wanted to drop the contract altogether, except for Allison's agreement not to use alcohol or other drugs. They wanted my "blessing."

Allison, who had grown at least two inches, started out the session with a big, gorgeous smile. "I'm here to make your day," she announced. "I'm not addicted." Of course, she was referring to the time I had invited her to make my day by telling me she was addicted. We both laughed and I assured her I couldn't be more delighted.

Phyllis and Stuart reported that Allison was out of the parochial school and back in her local high school, where she had wanted to be all along. She was involved in several extracurricular activities, had developed a caring relationship with her sister, and was usually friendly and warm toward her parents. Once again she was an honor student who associated with a nonusing crowd and was following the rules of the household.

Allison said she had no intention of drinking alcohol until she was of legal age. "Then we'll see. If I do drink, I'll go at it slowly, that's for sure."

Phyllis and Stuart reported that they saw absolutely no signs of the use of alcohol or any other drugs, and Allison appeared healthy and happy. Their plan to drop the contract was a healthy move.

You've already read about Brad's turbulent recovery, during which he was in and out of treatment for a couple of years. Now twenty-three, he has just celebrated his second AA anniversary, is living at home, and is going to college. It finally looks like he is making it.

According to Barbara, "Brad's turned into a real good kid. I always loved him because he was my son, but now I actually like him. If he doesn't make it this time, I know we'll be more devastated than ever. But we've been through a lot, and John and I have learned that we can survive no matter what Brad does. We're taking it a day at a time. Right now, it's wonderful having him back as a member of the family."

If you're about to give up hope for your child, consider Brad's history. As a young teenager, he was in a psychiatric hospital three times and in a school for emotionally disturbed adolescents for several months. Subsequently, he was jailed several times and, when not living on the streets, was in four chemical dependency treatment centers and three halfway houses. Now, finally, he is becoming stabilized in abstinence from chemicals and living in a way that works.

Mark is in his first year of college, where he remains active in AA. "I recouped my senior year in high school but wasn't able to get into Princeton. We pay a price for addiction, and that was mine. I'm only glad it wasn't worse. I'm happy with this school, grateful to be here and grateful to be alive."

Unlike Brad's recovery, Mark's was not turbulent, "just boring. It was real hard not using until I found a bunch of new friends in the AA program and a whole lot of things to do instead of getting high. Being a sports nut has been a saving grace. I've got a job as a guide at Outward Bound, and every vacation I take kids on clean and dry wilderness trips where we put ourselves to the test—you know, get in touch with our strengths and connect with nature and each other in a really close way. That keeps me on track for months.''

Mark reports he still is not tying the laces of his sneakers.

I hope Kimberly is out there—somewhere. She has not dropped by in several months.

As you may recall, David was not able to keep his no-chemical-use contract and was then admitted to an in-patient chemical dependency treatment center, where he did well. Following treatment, he returned to his mother's house and his former school. He attended AA meetings several times a week and stayed in recovery support group therapy throughout the remainder of his senior year of high school.

Now in his third year of college, majoring in Russian Studies, he's about to leave for Russia as an exchange student for six months. "It will be the first time that I'll be away from AA and I'm scared . . . but I think I'm prepared. I will call my sponsor every week, and I'm taking all my AA literature with me. Life is good now, and I don't want to blow it. If I have to call my sponsor every day, I'll call every day. My dad said he'd pick up the tab. If things get really bad, I can always come home. But I'm pretty sure I'll be okay.''

Once she discovered she had the AIDS virus, JoAnn refused to enter the extended-care facility suggested by the treatment center. Instead, she returned home and was drunk by the evening of her fourth day. Fortunately, her parents insisted that she return to treatment, where she participated in the program only reluctantly. Then she went to an extended care facility for six months. Upon her discharge, while at the airport with her parents, she excused herself, ostensibly to go to the ladies' room, and went to one of the bars, where she got plastered. Sue Ellen and Matt, their hearts breaking, once again escorted her back to the treatment center. "We were not about to give up on her, even though she had given up on herself," Sue Ellen reported.

"Thank God you didn't," added JoAnn. "This time I heard them in treatment. When they told me to fight it [AIDS], I finally heard them and began to believe I really could."

JoAnn's life will never be normal, not unless a drug is discovered that kills the AIDS virus. But her life today, nearly two years later, is full of meaning. She is clean and dry. She still has no symptoms of AIDS and is convinced she will remain free of the disease. She has become involved with holistic medicine, positive imagery, and a macrobiotic diet. "No way am I putting toxic stuff into my body. I'm beating the little buggers [AIDS viruses], and I'm helping others do the same."

At first, JoAnn worked at the AIDS hotline in her county. She is now actively involved with forming a support network for persons who carry the AIDS virus. "It's just like AA. We don't judge each other. We help each other one day at a time. I don't live tomorrow today. Maybe I'll never be able to get married and have children like other people, but then again, maybe I will. Who knows? Right now, I've got today, and today is pretty good."

Tim is still breathing, so there's hope, but things do not look good.

Following his intervention, he completed treatment at the chemical dependency center with flying colors and went on to a halfway house for six months. Soon after his discharge, he started using alcohol and drugs. For the past three years since then, he has been in and out of several detoxification hospitals, treatment centers, and halfway houses, but has never stayed off chemicals for more than a month when not confined.

Mary and Marty came to see me last week. They've done a really good job of taking care of themselves. Marty completed a month of in-patient treatment at a center for eating disorders, has lost close to eighty pounds, and is active in Overeaters Anonymous. Both remain active in Al-Anon and have received therapy for their sexual difficulties.

When Tim called last Sunday, Marty refused to speak to him, but Mary took the call. Tim said he was calling from a men's shelter in a city several states away, where he has been living for several years. He said that he needed to be detoxified but had no way to get to the hospital. Mary said that she was sorry but there was nothing she could do to help him, and suggested that he call the police.

The next day, Tim called from another men's shelter and said that he did call the police the day before, was taken to a hospital for detoxification, but was raped by three men and had to call the police to get out. Feeling the old pull to get involved, Mary called the police to check on Tim's story. Yes, indeed, the police had been called, but by the hospital, not by Tim. It seems that he had to be removed because he was tearing the place apart.

The next day, from yet another shelter, Tim called to say that he had just shot himself in the leg and if his parents didn't help him out, he was going to come home and shoot them both. Mary told him that she was not going to accept any more calls from him until he'd been sober for at least ninety days, and hung up.

"Isn't there anything we can do?" Mary asked.

"Like what?" I answered, feeling about as helpless as they must have felt. "Beyond protecting yourself from Tim should he return—which seems unlikely since he hasn't been home in years—what can you do? You're no longer supporting his addiction, and although you've offered treatment to him many times, he has not responded. I don't see anything else you can do.''

''What if we went to see him?'' Mary pleaded.

''Carry that thought through. You've already done that once; what do you imagine would happen this time?''

''I know what would happen, Mary, and so do you,'' Marty said. ''We'd end up giving into his crazy demands, just like we did the last time, and be right back into supporting his addiction again. If he really wants treatment, he knows how to get it himself. He doesn't need us, Mary. We can't help him. We've tried and tried and tried. Now we've got to let him go.''

And I agreed.

Chemical dependency is a serious illness. Not everyone recovers. Generally, the earlier the disease is recognized and treated, the greater the odds for recovery. But even with early recognition and treatment, some addicted adolescents and young adults have to be treated repeatedly. Even with repeated treatment, a few will not recover.

Treatment does not guarantee recovery, but it is the only option that offers that hope. Yes, there are kids who do not make it; who run away from treatment; who use after treatment; who overdose, attempt suicide, and die. But there are many victories, many kids who remain chemically free, who complete the maturative tasks of adolescence and put their lives together in ways that truly work. They would not be alive were it not for treatment.

Preventive Parenting

The dilemma of parenting is that no matter how much of our life we devote to our children, the results are in large part beyond our control.

We cannot control the inherent nature of our children, the individual characteristics and talents they bring into the world. We cannot prevent our children from being too short or too tall, from having learning disabilities or predispositions toward addiction and other illnesses. Nor can we protect them from extreme shyness or high-strung temperaments. And we cannot confer upon them optimism, stamina, sweet dispositions, and high IQs.

Nor can we completely control the nurture that we give our children, no matter how hard we try. Some of us, perhaps dealing with the shortcomings of our own upbringings, will fall short repeatedly. We may be overprotective, controlling, and afraid to let our children face frustration. We may try to force our children to achieve what eluded us. Or we may find our parenting energies preempted by events beyond our control, such as illness, divorce, or death. We certainly cannot prevent freak accidents, nor can we guarantee inspiring teachers and approving peers. We cannot even provide our children with a chemical-free environment.

We also cannot control the constant interplay between our children's nature and the nurture they receive. Although we may be role models of optimism, we cannot, for example, guarantee that a child handicapped in several significant ways will see his world optimistically, as Brian was able to. Nor can we make him persevere, as Brian did. Much as we would like, we cannot control our children's sense of self-worth and adequacy, although we can create an environment that nurtures self-esteem.

So much is beyond our control—what our children bring with them into the world, what the world brings to our children, what our children do with their world. Nevertheless, what happens in childhood matters a lot and, as parents, we are its primary engineers.

Two surveys conducted over a ten-month period in 1986 and 1987 by the *Minneapolis Star and Tribune*—a survey of 5,473 suburban St. Paul/Minneapolis students in grades eight, ten, and twelve and a poll of 386 school alcohol/drug specialists— showed that when it comes to alcohol and other drug use, it matters little whether teenagers are rich or poor, in public or private schools, in extracurricular activities or not. What does matter is the *family*.

Teenagers who do not use alcohol, or other drugs, or whose use of alcohol is appreciably low, report good family relationships and none-to-moderate parental drinking. Their parents are strict but approachable, keep a close watch on them, and forbid them to drink alcohol or use other drugs.

On the other hand, teenagers who are serious users of alcohol or other drugs are three times more likely to come from single-parent homes than are nonusers. They report less family closeness. Their parents are not very strict, are half as likely as parents of nonusers to take alcohol and other drug use seriously, have unclear expectations about chemical use, are heavy drinkers or users of other drugs, and let their children out many nights a week without supervision. These findings coincide with what I have found in my work with suburban youth in the greater New York area, and they match what many of my colleagues across the country report at conferences.

Preventive parenting does not guarantee no-to-low chemical use among teenagers, but it helps. Let's examine some of the factors involved in preventive parenting.

Role Modeling

Children who develop harmful involvements with chemicals often—not always, but often—have parents who are harmfully involved with chemicals. If you do not believe me, go to an open AA meeting. You will find a room full of people, about 60 percent of whom swore they would never ever drink like their alcoholic parent. And there they are. We simply cannot escape the fact that if our chemical use is aberrant, we are setting our children up for the same.

Though not addicted, many of the parents with whom I work nevertheless demonstrate aberrant chemical use. Du Pont Corporation used to have a slogan: "Better Living Through Chemistry." Dupont has dropped this slogan, but many parents have picked it up. Some rush out for antibiotics at their child's first sneeze. Others give their child aspirin or its equivalent, as if it were a panacea for all woes. Altogether too many parents pop Valium routinely to calm their nerves. Others smoke marijuana, then wonder why their kids attempt to alter their state of consciousness with LSD or crack. Many have a martini or a beer the moment they walk in the door at the end of the workday in order to relax, then complain when their child smokes a joint after a hard day at school.

These parents are giving a powerful message to their children: that life really is lived better through chemistry. They will not be able to suddenly erase this message once their children approach adolescence. In fact, they may find their message indelibly engraved on their child's psyche.

If we drink and then drive, for example, how can we expect our children not to do the same? Or if we drink and become intoxicated—even once—how can we avoid giving our children the message that getting drunk is to some degree permissible? Even worse, if we drink and become intoxicated with some degree of regularity, as some parents do, then not only do we stand the chance of losing our children's respect, we stand the chance of losing our ability to influence them positively in other areas of their lives.

On the other hand, we can go too far in the opposite direction. Parents who abstain from alcohol for health reasons or because they do not like it have been shown to be good role models for their children, while parents who abstain for moral reasons, or who are fanatic about abstinence, are less effective. Too often an alcohol-phobic or moralistic stance makes alcohol seem as irresistible as the apple in the Garden of Eden.

So what *is* safe behavior? Of course, nothing is guaranteed. However, as the surveys show, children who do not use alcohol or other drugs or who drink moderate amounts on occasion have parents who do the same. If the parents drink alcohol, it is often a glass or two of wine or beer used to enhance special occasions like birthdays, holidays, graduations, and other celebrations.

That's it? I'm afraid so. *Apples fall near the tree.* If you want your children to be abstainers or only occasional moderate alcohol users, then that is how you should behave.

Role modeling is not mindless imitation, nor is it intimidation. Rather, role modeling means that our children are sufficiently impressed to want to act like us, think like us, or live as we do. Toni, Brian, and, once sober, Mark, Allison, David, and JoAnn spoke of how impressed they were with the lives their parents were leading and the kind of people they were. True, their parental modeling hadn't prevented harmful chemical involvements, yet all eventually made healthy decisions regarding their chemical use, *in part because of a desire to be more like their parents*. That's how role modeling works. Parents set examples that the children can try out, bit by bit, seeing if they feel inherently good or whether they lead to external rewards.

Adolescents use their parents as yardsticks—tools for measuring themselves—which are composites of perceived values, beliefs, attitudes, and behavioral skills. The imaginary yardsticks serve as a familiar point of reference to which teenagers can turn to see how they are "measuring up" in their quest for independence and maturity. They can return to it, time after time, for a sense of direction, groundedness, and guidance.

We parents often believe that we lose our ability to influence through role modeling once children become teenagers. We are quick to point to peer influence, or assume that parental rejection is a natural part of growing up. We speak of the generation gap, how arguments replace conversations, and how simple rules of the household are repeatedly challenged. Often it seems as if our primary function has been reduced to supplying allowances, room and board, and telephone answering services. To some degree, this is true; our ability to influence our children is reduced once they become adolescents. But it is far from eliminated.

First, adolescents are at school or with friends much of the time, but they are home a lot, too, so ample opportunity for parental role modeling persists. Second, children are exposed to parental role modeling throughout their growing years, so it remains extremely influential. Third, until children reach adulthood, parents are the principal authority figures. Parents may not believe it, but they still matter profoundly to their teenage children. Because they matter, parents have a continuing influence.

Role modeling comes in all forms. At its best, it is a program of attraction, whereby examples set by parents lead to positive results when tried out by their children. The more parents "walk their own talk," or live as they want their children to live, the more influence they will have with their teenagers.

At its worst, role modeling is a program of hypocrisy, where parents "play by their own rules," which change according to circumstances. They insist that their children "do as I say, not as I do." Teenagers despise phoniness. Hypocritical role modeling can lead teenagers to a distrust of all adults or to problems in school, simply because they cannot believe their teachers actually mean what they say. It may encourage children to rebel against all authority, or to abandon attempts at self-control and to give in to delinquent behavior—alcohol and other drug abuse, sexual promiscuity, truancy, crime. The more teenagers perceive parental hypocrisy in action, the less influential their parents will be in their lives, at least in a positive sense.

Love in a Physical Way

In the abstract, love does not seem very real to a child. One young man, a high school junior in the early stage of his recovery from chemical dependency, said he "guessed" that his parents "probably" loved him. He wasn't too sure; he rarely saw them. His father was a surgeon who kept long work hours; days would go by without their paths crossing. His mother, an archeologist, spent weeks or even months away on digs.

To love a child, we have to be *physically present* at least some of the time. Deborah, Toni's mother, traveled on business several times a year and always experienced misgivings about it. "People would try to make me feel better by telling me it was quality time that mattered, not quantity time," she said. "But I never bought it; I knew both were important. I handled it the best I could. I traveled only when it was absolutely necessary and, whenever possible, took my children with me, usually one at a time."

Most importantly, according to Toni, when her mother "was there, she was *really* there. She wasn't just sitting around, she was doing things with us. We'd get her involved in all our crazy projects, from outrageous Halloween costumes to tramping in the woods looking for different kinds of moss for our science class. And when we were performing at school, in a play or something, she'd be sitting in the audience, beaming. My mom hugs us a lot, but I want to tell you, when she shines one of those beams at you, you know you're loved.

"Talking with her was always easy. We didn't get the interrogations, you know. It was more natural. My mom would tell us about her day, or we'd tell her about ours. There was a lot of sharing. But like I said, she was there in ways that were annoying as hell, too. Like doing all that calling to make sure we'd be places where parents were home and alcohol was not being served. And she'd wait up for us, too, for the goodnight kiss.

"Once . . . this was funny. One night my sister and I were each having a friend sleep over, and the four of us went to a party and drank some beer. We all knew we couldn't have much because we had to get past my mom, so we probably only had a can, if that. On the way home, we rehearsed—actually rehearsed—how we'd kiss my mom so she wouldn't smell us. Our friends rehearsed, too, because my mom kisses our friends. So we walked in, gave her a quick buzz, told her we were tired, and went to bed, certain we'd gotten away with it. The next morning, while flipping the pancakes and passing the juice, she asked my friends who was going to tell their parents we'd been drinking, her or them. We almost had apoplexy! I wanted to die, I was so embarrassed. But my friends ended up calling their parents, and my sister and I got grounded and lost our phone privileges. My mom didn't let us get away with much.''

Brian's parents and Mark's father showed their love in other tangible ways as well, most importantly through active listening and shared activities. Some parents—in fact, many of those I work with—do not. It's as if they have lost touch with the child within them. They don't seem to value what their children have to say, or even appreciate their children's feelings. And they don't seem to know how to be silly, how to frolic in the waves, build a snowman, or put a worm on a hook. When they listen, it's often only when they read the newspaper or watch television. They do not give their child their undivided attention. And when they play, it's work; winning is all, fun irrelevant. Yet, of the two, it's shared fun, not winning, that stands the best chance of bringing parents and children together.

Children have a need for love to be demonstrated consistently, *so that they can depend on it*. One of the most extreme lacks of consistency occurs in families where one or both of the parents is alcoholic. At best, the children have a parent who is involved some of the time, but not at other times. It depends largely on whether the parent is drunk or sober. Without a consistent demonstration of physical love, children grow up feeling unloved, confused, and untrusting.

When love is consistently demonstrated in a tangible way, children experience a sense of family closeness, which is a very important part of preventive parenting. If we want our attitudes about alcohol and other drugs to outweigh those of our children's chemical-using peers, we have to provide our children with an environment in which good feelings, or the "highs" associated with family closeness, outweigh those associated with chemicals.

Commitment to Action

In addition to feeling close to their families, children who do not use chemicals report that their parents are strict, do not let them go out many evenings during the school week, always know where they are, and make efforts to ensure that their parties are chaperoned and chemical-free—all of which takes considerable effort.

The kids complain. "You don't trust me." "Other parents don't call to see if alcohol is going to be served or not." "Why do you always have to embarrass me?" "Why can't I go out during the week? Everyone else can." But these parents stand firm. To help our children resist the use of alcohol and other drugs, we parents need to be action-oriented. We need to keep ourselves informed about our children's activities; we need to set rules and stand by them.

We need, in other words, to be "nerds." *Our children do not need us as friends.* They need us as parents—friendly, but not friends—loving, concerned, and informed authority figures prepared to take the actions necessary to help them further their own best interests.

Brian said he hated his dad's reaction when Paul found out that he was doing dope. "But even at the time, I knew he was right and that he had flipped because he cared about me. I used to feel sorry for some of the kids I knew. Their parents didn't seem to care what they did. One of my friends got so drunk one night he passed out in a snowbank on the way home and nearly froze to death. He had to have some toes amputated, and his parents never even told him to stop drinking.

"But my parents showed they cared in a lot of other ways,

too. I mean, they knew what we were into and supported our interests. My mom would go out of her way to get concert tickets for me, and when my brother wanted a computer, my mom started a computer fund. That's what she'd do for the special things we couldn't afford. Whoever's fund it was would be responsible for kicking in some of his earnings, and my parents would also contribute weekly. Sometimes it seemed to take forever, but it worked. That's how we got the really special things we wanted.''

Brian reported that vacations were also very much a family matter. Every year they selected a country they wanted to visit, then advertised their house in various travel magazines in exchange for the house of a family from that country. ''My parents don't have as much money as others in my town, but we've never had to go without the things that really mattered to us, and we've had better vacations than just about anybody. Name it, we've been there: Brazil, Ireland, Australia, Scotland, France, Japan, Panama. Every year a new country. We all fish, and we all scuba dive. And we all like being in different cultures and trying out different kinds of foods. So we always picked a place where we could be near water at least some of the time, and we tried to make it as different as possible each year. Vacations are a little tamer now because so much money is going into our education, but we're still at it. This summer we're going down to Key West. Maybe that's not the greatest place to be in the summer, or the most exciting, but we'll all be together and the fishing and diving will be great.''

Brian claimed that he never used pot after the night his father charged into the auditorium, but he admitted that he still drank ''every once in a while. But I want to tell you that my dad really put a damper on the whole thing. My parents waited up for me or got up to say good night—so if I was bombed, they'd see it for sure. Dad really took the fun out of drinking. I mean, now I'm okay with it, but back then I wasn't. Every time I picked up a drink, I knew I was doing something wrong, something I knew he didn't want me to do. I loved my dad. His approval meant a lot to me.''

When asked to pick one word to describe each of his parents, Brian did not hesitate. His mom was *involved* and his dad was *strict*. ''They went out of their way to know what was going on with us and to do things with us. They knew what we were studying and how we were doing. They came to our games and all that, so they were both *actively* involved in our lives. My dad's rules held, no matter what. We never could go out at night during the week unless it was a special school activity, and we had to be in by one on Friday and Saturday. Most of my friends didn't even have curfews and they could go out during the week, too, but my dad only cared about us and what he thought was right.''

When asked if there was anything he would change in the way he was raised, Brian answered, ''Well, one thing maybe. My dad was so rigid. Sometimes I had a really good case . . . like a good reason why I should have been able to stay out beyond my curfew, but Dad was pretty inflexible. He had a hard time seeing he wasn't always right.

''Once he did bend. Sometime in my first or second year of high school, my dad told me he'd give me fifty dollars for each A I brought home. At first, it sounded good. I really wanted that money. But I couldn't get A's. No way! I got depressed after that, really down. It was like my brothers were good enough for him, but I wasn't. That hurt, especially because they got A's but I was the one who studied the most.

''What finally happened was my coach talked to me. I guess he could see something was wrong. I wasn't even sure what was wrong, but when I told the coach that my dad wanted me to get A's and I was having a hard time getting C's, everything crystallized. My coach helped me to see that C's for me were like A's for my brothers, something to be celebrated, not knocked.

"The coach was great. We went over it several times, you know, sorta like strategy for a game. Finally I was able to talk to my dad about it, and he really came through for me. He said he agreed with me. My dad actually admitted that he was wrong and I was right. Man, that felt good! I think that's another reason I felt so bad about drinking. I mean, my dad was there for me when I needed him, and there I was doing stuff I knew he was against.

"When I was in college and had to go to the dean, my dad helped me out again. It was Thanksgiving and that Friday before going back to school, I got a special delivery letter telling me I was suspended and not to come back. My dad didn't put me down at all. He just asked me what I wanted to do, and when I told him I wanted to talk to the dean, he took off from work and went back to school with me. My dad didn't actually go into the dean's office with me—that I had to do alone—but I knew he was behind me all the way. I'm not too sure I could've done that without his support. So you see, that's what I mean when I say I'm lucky. Along with everything else, I've got great parents."

Another important way we can help our children is through problem solving—that is, through effective handling of family crises. Some parents simply are not prepared to take action, not even the first step of getting themselves informed. As we have seen with Ramona and Jim, and Mary and Marty, living with and being victimized by an addicted child long enough virtually ensures parental paralysis. But other parents, many of whom were themselves victimized as children of dysfunctional parents, also tend to revert to a state of powerlessness in times of crisis. When action is called for, they often feel helpless and immobilized. Knowing this about themselves, or finding out the hard way, many adult children of dysfunctional parents today are seeking treatment so that, among other things, they can be more effective parents.

If we manage crises successfully, we can come out of them emotionally strengthened. When families work through problems together, the whole family is emotionally reinforced. Furthermore, along with learning coping skills, our children learn that most important of lessons: problems can be solved. And they learn that lesson through *doing*, our most potent means of learning.

A large number of parents across the United States are now recognizing that it is difficult singlehandedly to ban alcohol and other drugs from their children's lives. To create a chemical-free environment for their children, they are working through churches, community groups, and PTAs to form a united front, to lay down common rules, and to strictly enforce them. In many communities parents are forming ''safe homes,'' designated homes where teenage parties are chaperoned and are chemical-free.

Such informed, united parental action can go far. Kids have been united all along. It is time now for parents to be united against adolescent alcohol and other drug use.

Presently our children live in a chemical-using environment where they face alcohol and other drugs every day of the week, one way or another. They need action-oriented parents: parents prepared to become informed; parents prepared to take appropriate action; parents prepared to intervene in their chemical use.

Clearly Stated
Expectations and Consequences

Most parents are unequivocally opposed to the use of co-caine, heroin, PCP, angel dust, LSD, and other illegal drugs with a dangerous reputation. Some parents, however, are ambivalent about marijuana or actually believe that adolescent use of alcohol is safe. These feelings may cause parents to refrain from stating any expectations or consequences at all, or to make vague, unclear statements like, "Don't get drunk." "Don't drink too much." "Stick to the beer." "Stay away from the hard stuff." "If you're determined to smoke pot, at least don't drink at the same time." The only thing such ambiguous statements make clear is that drinking, and perhaps smoking pot, is, to some degree, permissible. Since both are illegal for teenagers, parents in essence are condoning breaking the law.

Children who do not use alcohol and other drugs, or whose use is minimal, cite parental reasons—namely, that *their parents forbid it*.

Adolescents, especially those with close family ties, value parental expectations. They are inclined to meet them. But to be able to meet them, the expectations must first be extremely clear. The most helpful thing we can do for our children is to forbid them not to use any drugs.

As previously discussed, adolescents need externally imposed limits in order to develop inner controls. Clearly stated parental expectations of no chemical use (other than a glass of wine, beer, or champagne at weddings, holiday gatherings, or religious services) provide these limits. Very simply, it is easier for children to say no when their parents expect it and when they know they will pay a price if they do not say no. The pressures our children face are enormous. By laying down the law, we give our children the ammunition to help fight the pressures they face. They can say, "I can't drink," or "I'll be grounded [or whatever] if I do."

Recall what children learn when they drink alcohol or use other drugs—that it makes them feel good, every time, immediately, and without any effort. Parents can affect that learning by making sure they exact a price for alcohol and other drug use. We can make alcohol and other drugs less enticing by imposing meaningful consequences.

Toni paid a price, a broken ankle, for her use of alcohol. She did not need any further punishment. Later, when Deborah smelled alcohol on her breath, Toni was grounded and had to give up her use of the phone for one week, a meaningful price indeed for a socially active sixteen-year-old. Once Brian's use of marijuana was discovered, he was grounded and asked to give up either hockey or music for two weeks. When one son ended up in the overnight holding pen at the local jail for driving while intoxicated, his father left him there, saying, "You got yourself in, you can get yourself out." Very wisely, he allowed his son to pay the legal price rather than imposing one of his own.

While it is important that the consequences be meaningful, it is also important that they be reasonable and of relatively brief duration; one to two weeks, for example. Anything much longer can make the consequence seem particularly unjust, and the child will then concentrate on the unfairness, and what he perceives as parental irrationality, rather than his own behavior.

It is also important that parents be calm. Most of us are furious when our child breaks a rule, but consequences are much more effective if imposed after a cooling-off period. If we pass judgment at the height of our anger—when we are at least partially out of control—we run the risk of seeming not only irrational but also unapproachable. In the future our children may be afraid to approach us when they have done something we do not approve of. Furthermore, we are apt to lay the excess baggage of our anger on the consequence, making it unduly harsh. In so doing, we shift the focus to our behavior, rather than the child's.

It is best if the consequences are agreed upon by both parties in advance. Then, even though they know they will pay a price for drinking, the children acknowledge in advance that it is reasonable and that it will be rationally imposed. As a result, the chances are good that if they've been drinking, for example, the children will not be too afraid to call home for a ride rather than drive themselves.

Pass by your local elementary school any afternoon toward the end of the school day. Pause a few moments. Look at all those carefree little creatures skipping about in their colorful clothes. Look hard. They are our most valuable resource.

Look at the older ones, the sixth graders. Ask yourself if you truly believe alcohol is safe for their developing minds, bodies, and souls. One-third of them are already experimenting with alcohol, and pressure is on for all of them. Ask yourself if they are old enough to withstand that pressure without your help, or old enough to decide wisely.

Look a final time. Realize that, as things stand today, unless parents take a solid, united stand against adolescent and preadolescent drinking, one out of three of those carefree little creatures will manifest alcohol problems by the time they become seniors. Know that. It's true.

Now look inward, to yourself; then outward, to other parents. The answers lie with us, not our children.

It simply is not enough for us to tell our kids to say no. We have to *help* them say no—no to alcohol and no to all other drugs.

Children will say no if we help them to.

APPENDICES

Appendix A

Self-Help Programs for Parents

Al-Anon
1372 Broadway
New York, NY 10018
(212) 302-7240

Drug-Anon
P.O. Box 473
Ansonia Station
New York, NY 10023
(212) 874-0700

Families Anonymous
P.O. Box 528
Van Nuys, CA 91408

Toughlove
P.O. Box 1069
Doylestown, PA 18901
(215) 348-7090

Self-Help Programs for Addicted Adolescents

Alcoholics Anonymous
P.O. Box 459
Grand Central Station
New York, NY 10163
(212) 686-1100

Drugs Anonymous
P.O. Box 473
Ansonia Station, NY 10023
(212) 874-0700

Self-Help Programs for Addicted Adolescents (cont.)

Cocaine Anonymous
P.O. Box 1367
Culver City, CA 90232

Also look in your telephone directory for local chapters of these groups.

Appendix B

Treatment Referral Resources

BOOKS:

National Directory of Drug Abuse and Alcoholism Treatment and Prevention Programs. Published by the National Clearinghouse for Drug and Alcohol Information, P.O. Box 2345, Rockville, MD, 20852 (301) 468-2600. This directory also should be available in the reference section of your library.

Rehab: A Comprehensive Guide to Recommended Drug-Alcohol Treatment Centers in the U.S. By Stan Hart. Published by Harper & Row, 1988.

The 100 Best Treatment Centers for Alcoholism and Drug Abuse. By Linda Sunshine and John Wright. Published by Avon Books, 1988.

ORGANIZATIONS:

Joint Commission on Accreditation of Hospitals (JCAH)
875 North Michigan Avenue
Chicago, IL 60611
(312) 642-6061

National Association of Alcohol and Drug Abuse Counselors, Inc. (NAADAC)
3717 Columbia Pike, Suite 300
Arlington, VA 22204
(703) 920-4644

ORGANIZATIONS (cont.):

National Council on Alcoholism
12 West 21st Street
New York, NY 10010
(212) 206-6770
(Local branches are listed in the
White Pages)

Therapeutic Communities of
America
54 West 40th Street
New York, NY 10018
(212) 354-6000

OTHER SOURCES:
In the telephone directory, look under "Alcoholism Information and
Treatment," "Drug Abuse and Addiction Information and Treat-
ment," and "Chemical Dependency Information and Treatment."

Appendix C

Hotlines

Cocaine Hotline: (800) COC-AINE
National Adolescent Suicide Hotline: (800) 621-4000
National Institute on Drug Abuse Helpline: (800) 662-HELP
National Parents' Resource Institute for Drug Education Drug In-
formation Line: (404) 577-4500
Parents' Association to Neutralize Drug and Alcohol Abuse, The
Listening Ear: (703) 750-9285

Appendix D

Parent Action/Education Associations

Families in Action
National Drug Information Center
3845 North Druid Hills Road, Suite 300
Decatur, GA 30033
(404) 325-5799

The Just Say No Foundation
177 North California Boulevard, Suite 200
Walnut Creek, CA 94596
(800) 258-2766
(414) 939-6666

Mothers Against Drunk Driving (MADD)
669 Airport Freeway, Suite 310
Hurst, TX 76053
(817) 268-MADD

Parents' Association to Neutralize Drug and Alcohol Abuse
P.O. Box 314
Annandale, VA 22003
(703) 750-9285

National Parents' Resource Institute for Drug Education (PRIDE)
50 Hurt Plaza, Suite 210
Atlanta, GA 30303
(404) 577-4500

Bibliography

Allison, Russel. *Drug Abuse: Why It Happens and How to Prevent It.* Lower Burrel, PA: Valley Publishing, 1983.

Baron, Jason D. *Kids & Drugs: A Parent's Handbook of Drug Abuse Prevention.* New York: Perigee Books, 1981.

Barun, Ken, and Philip Basher. *When Saying No Isn't Enough: How To Keep the Children You Love Off Drugs.* New York: New American Library, 1988.

Beattie, Melody. *Codependent No More.* Center City, MN: Hazelden, 1987.

Bell, Ruth, and Leni Zeiger Wildflower. *Talking with Your Teenager.* New York: Random House, 1983.

Chatlos, Calvin. *Crack: What You Should Know about the Cocaine Epidemic.* New York: Perigee Books, 1987.

Chilnick, Lawrence D. (ed.). *The Little Black Pill Book.* New York: Bantam Books, 1983.

Claypool, Jane Miner. *Alcohol and Teens.* New York: Messner, 1984.

Cohen, Susan, and Daniel Cohen. *Teenage Stress.* New York: Evans, 1984.

Cretcher, Dorothy. *Steering Clear: Helping Your Child Through the High-Risk Drug Years.* San Francisco: Winston Press, 1982.

Donlan, Joan. *I Never Saw the Sun Rise: The Diary of a Recovering Chem-*

ically Dependent Teenager. Minneapolis: CompCare Publications, 1977.

Dupont, Robert L., Jr. *Getting Tough on Gateway Drugs*. Washington, DC: American Psychiatric Publishing, 1984.

Esman, Aaron H. *The Psychology of Adolescence*. New York: International Universities Press, 1975.

Gold, Mark S. *The Facts about Drugs and Alcohol*. New York: Bantam Books, 1986.

Hart, Stan. *Rehab: A Comprehensive Guide to Recommended Drug-Alcohol Treatment Centers in the United States*. New York: Harper & Row, 1988.

Hyden, Nancy Woodward. *If Your Child Is Drinking . . .* New York: Putnam, 1981.

Johnson, Vernon. *Intervention: How to Help Someone Who Doesn't Want Help*. Minneapolis: Johnson Institute Publications, 1987.

Kolodny, Robert C., Nancy J. Kolodny, Thomas Bratter, and Cheryl Deep. *How to Survive Your Adolescent's Adolescence*. Boston: Little, Brown, 1984.

Krupnick, Louis, and Elizabeth Krupnick. *From Despair to Decision*. Minneapolis: CompCare Publications, 1985.

Manthe, George L. *Inside Dope*. Port Jefferson, New York: Cube Publications, 1983.

Maxwell, Ruth. *Beyond the Booze Battle*. New York: Ballantine, 1986.

———*The Booze Battle*. New York: Ballantine, 1976.

National Directory of Drug Abuse and Alcoholism Treatment and Prevention Programs. Washington, DC: National Institute of Drug Abuse, 1984.

Neff, Pauline. *Tough Love: How Parents Can Deal with Drug Abuse*. Nashville: Abingdon, 1982.

Otteson, Orlo, John Townsend, Ph.D., and Tim Rumsey, M.D. *Kids & Drugs: A Parent's Guide*. New York: CFS Publishing Corp., 1983.

Physician's Desk Reference. 40th ed. Oradell, NJ: Medical Economics Company, 1986.

Polson, Beth, and Miller Newton, Ph.D. *Not My Kid: A Parent's Guide to Kids and Drugs*. New York: Arbor House Publishing Co., 1984.

Russell, George K. *Marijuana Today: A Compilation of Medical Findings.* The Myrin Institute, 1978.

Schaefer, Dick. *Choices and Consequences: What to Do When a Teenager Uses Alcohol/Drugs.* Minneapolis: Johnson Institute Books, 1984.

Scott, Sharon. *PPR: Peer Pressure Reversal: How to Say No and Keep Your Friends.* Amherst, MA: Human Resource Development Press, 1986.

Sunshine, Linda, and John W. Wright. *The 100 Best Treatment Centers for Alcoholism and Drug Abuse.* New York: Avon Books, 1988.

Van Ost, William C., M.D., and Elaine Van Ost. *Warning Signs—A Parent's Guide to In-time Intervention in Drug and Alcohol Abuse.* New York: Warner Books, 1988.

York, Phyllis, and David York. *Toughlove: A Self-Help Manual for Parents Troubled by Teenage Behavior.* Doylestown, PA: Toughlove International, 1980.

Youcha, Geraldine, and Judith S. Seixas. *Drugs, Alcohol and Your Children.* New York: Avon, 1988.

INDEX

Action, parental commitment to, 209–13

Addiction
  and behavior, 10
  and defense mechanisms, 156
  definition of, 7
  degrading aspects of, 167
  and denial, 120–21
  early stages, 9
  late-stage, characteristics, 157
  relationship with chemicals in, 8–9
  urge to get high in, 7–8

Addiction specialist, screening
    questions
    for, 117

Adolescents
  choices and contemporary life, 40–42
  disturbed behavior of, 22–23
  maturational tasks of, 13–14
  negative dependency stage, 14
  and parental conflict, 41
  peaceful period of, 22
  peer groups, 24–33
  and personality structure, 81, 83
  physical changes, 21

Advertisements, and alcohol/drug
    use, 48

AIDS, 187, 197–98

Al-Anon, 83, 142

Alcohol, 60–63
  and tobacco use, 63–64
  as cause of death, 60
  as drug of choice, 43
  early use and addiction, 62
  effects of early use, 43
  functioning and later teen years, 62–63
  and growing bodies, 61
  physiological effects of, 61
  and preadolescents, 61–62, 63
  statistics on use, 42

Alcohol/drugs
  consistent effects of, 58–59
  reasons for use, 47–49, 50–51, 55
  signs of use, 90–103
  use as normal event, 50

Alcoholics Anonymous, 125

Ambivalence about chemicals,
    parental, 203–4, 214

Amotivational syndrome, and
    marijuana, 65

Amphetamines, 67
  physiological effects, 67
  types of, 67

Angel dust, 70

Antidepressants, in treatment, 126

Autonomy, adolescence, 13–14

Availability, and alcohol/drug use,
    48–49

Benzedrine, 67
Blackouts, 54
Butyl nitrite, 66

Chemical dependency
   as cause of emotional illness, 74,
      114–16
   definition of, 7
   multiple drug use, 9–10
   as progressive disease, 167–68
Chemical dependency units, 125
China White, 71
Chloral hydrate, 70
Choices, and contemporary life, 40–
   42
Cocaine, 60, 67–68
   combined with heroin, 70
   cost of, 67
   death from, 68
   euphoria of, 68
   line/hit, meaning of, 67
   paraphernalia for, 67
   physiological effects of, 68
   psychological effects of, 68
   routes of administration, 67
   source of, 67
   time factors in addiction, 68
Cocaine Anonymous, 125
Codeine, 70
Codependency. See Parental
   codependency
Consequences, effective use of, 215–
   16
Contemporary life, and choices, 40–
   42
Contract, 145–56
   example of, 154–55
   versus household rules, 160–61
   parents participation in, 146–47
   purpose of, 145–46, 156
   responsible behavior and privileges,
      149, 155
Cooperation of addicted teen
   with treatment, 123–24
   and treatment plan, 158–63
Cost factors, treatment options, 128
Crack, 49, 60, 69
   addictive quality of, 69
   cost of, 69

euphoria of, 69
production of, 69
use by middle class, 69

Defense mechanisms, and addiction,
   156
Death
   cocaine use, 68
   heroin use, 70
   and withdrawal, 122
Demerol, 70
Denial, 164
   and addiction, 120–21
   degree of and treatment needs, 123
   by parents, 105–9
Depression, 78
Designer drugs, 71–72
   Ecstasy, 71, 72
   methamphetamine, 71
Dexedrine, 67
Dilaudid, 70
Disengagement, from parental
   codependency, 143
Dopamine, 68
Drive to get high, nature of, 7–8
Dropouts, 47
Drugs of choice
   alcohol, 60–63
   tobacco, 63–64
   designer drugs, 71–72
      Ecstasy, 71, 72
      methamphetamine, 71
   heroin, 70
   inhalants, 66
   marijuana, 64–66
   miscellaneous drugs, 70–71
   stimulants, 66–69
      amphetamines, 67
      cocaine, 67–68
      crack, 69

Early use and addiction, alcohol, 62
Ecstasy, 71, 72
Emotional illness, chemical
   dependency as cause, 74, 114–
   16
Enabling role, parents, 168
Euphoria
   degree of and addiction, 72

Euphoria, *(continued)*
 and drug use, 51
Expectations of parents, clarity of,
 214–16
Experimentation, 47
Extended-care facilities, 127, 128

Families Anonymous, 83, 142
Family
 family characteristic of nonusers,
  202
 family characteristics of heavy
  users, 202
 home environment and treatment,
  127
Family crisis, and problem solving,
 212–13
Family system, effects of addicted
 member on, 139–40
Fentanyl, 71
Freebasing, 56

Guilt, parental, 138

Halfway houses, 125, 127, 128
Heroin, 29–31, 70
 combined with cocaine, 70
 euphoria of, 70
 increase in use of, 70
 physiological effects, 70
 routes of administration, 70
 time span and addiction, 70
Home environment, and treatment,
 127
Hospitalization, 45–46
Hotlines, referral sources, 219

Ice, 71
Inhalants, 66
 euphoric effects of, 66
 physiological effects of, 66
 and preadolescents, 66
 types of, 66
In-patient treatment, 125, 126
 components of, 165
 criteria for use, 166
 family week, 165
 motivational aspects of, 165
 patient's refusal to stay, 182–84

 program of, 126
 refusal of teen to attend, 166
Insurance coverage, treatment, 128
Interventions. *See* Structured
 intervention
Isolation from family, 77–78

Johnston, Lloyd, 43

Locker Room, 66
Love
 and action, 79
 consistency in, 208
 demonstration of, 206–8
LSD, 70

Marijuana, 64–66
 and amotivational syndrome, 65
 cancerous effects of, 65
 physical appearance of, 64
 physiological effects of, 65
 potency of, 64
 and THC, 64, 65
MDMA. *See* Ecstasy
Mescaline, 70
Methadone maintenance, 130
Methamphetamine, 71
Miltown, 71
Moralistic stance, parental, 204
Morphine, 70
MPTP, 72
Multiple drug use, 9–10, 71
Mushrooms, 70

Narcotics Anonymous, 125
Nembutal, 70
Noctec, 70
Nonengagement, 78
Nonmodification, 78
Nontraditional families, 41

*The 100 Best Treatment Centers in the
 United States* (Sunshine and
 Wright), 129
Out-patient facilities, 125,
 126

Pain
 and addiction, 156

masking with alcohol/drugs, 55, 56–57

Paragoric, 70

Parent action/education associations, 220

Parental codependency, 132–43, 164, 168
  behaviors in, 136–38
  and degree of addiction, 140
  disengagement, 143
  distancer role in, 139
  feelings related to, 132, 133, 134, 136
  origins of, 136–42
  pursuer role in, 139
  recovery from, 184–86
  therapeutic intervention for, 142–43
  and treatment, 127

Parents
  ambivalent messages about chemicals, 203–4, 214
  denial of child's addiction, 105–9
  enabling role, 168
  feeling related to child's addiction, 10
  parental conflict and adolescence, 41
  reactions to substance use, 3–5
  self-help groups, 83
  attitudes about chemicals, effects of, 50–51

Parties, 48–49

PCP, 70

Peer group, 24–33
  and alcohol/drug use, 24–25
  effects of unhealthy group, 33
  positive influence of, 28, 31–33

Percodan, 70

Personality changes, 34, 35, 36, 37–40, 45, 46, 52–53, 111
  behavior/personality changes related to addiction (chart), 84–88
  depression, 78
  friendship with troubled peers, 78
  hostility, increased, 78
  ignored by parents, 79
  isolation from family, 77–78

nonengagement, 78
nonmodification, 78
parental evaluation of, 81–84

Personality structure, and adolescents, 81, 83

Physical changes, adolescents, 21

Preventive parenting, 201–16
  clear expectations and consequences of, 214–16
  commitment to action, 209–13
  family characteristic of nonusers, 202
  forbidding alcohol/drug use, 214–15
  love, demonstration of, 206–8
  role modeling, 203–6

PRIDE (Parents' Resource Institute for Drug Education), 42

Problem solving, and family crisis, 212–13

Psilicybin, 70

Psychiatric hospitals, chemical dependency unit, 125

Psychotherapy, and addictions, 117–18

Quaalude, 70

Rebellion, and alcohol/drug use, 47–48

Recovery, 188–200
  breaking abstinence rule, 191–92
  difficulty of, 189
  parental involvement in, 191
  and parental support, 192
  stages of, 189–90
  and trust, 192

Rehab (Hart), 129

Rock music, and alcohol/drug use, 48

Role modeling
  hypocritical role modeling, 206
  meaning of, 204–5
  parental, 203–6

Rush, 66

Sanorex, 67

Seconal, 70

Self-control, 49–50
  assessment of, 123
  and treatment needs, 123

Self-help groups, 125, 128
 contact information, 217–18
 for parents, 83
 types of, 125
Sexuality, 40, 41
Shame-based therapy, avoiding, 129–
 30
Signs of use, 90–103
 physical signs, 91, 92
 questioning school and, 97, 100
 searching child's room for, 91, 100
 signs of known/suspected alcohol
  and drug use (chart), 101–3
 See also Personality changes
Smith, Dr. David E., 60
Somnos, 70
Speed, 67
Speedball, 71
Stimulants
 amphetamines, 67
 cocaine, 67–68
 crack, 69
 side effects of, 66–67
Structured intervention, 164–87
 dialog in, 175–82
 effectiveness of, 166–67, 169
 parental fears in, 168
 rehearsal of team, 172–74
 team of persons for, 166, 174–
  75
Suicide, as parental fear, 168

Therapeutic communities, 125,
 127
Tobacco, 63–64
 and alcohol use, 63–64
 physiological effects of, 64
 social acceptance of, 63
Toughlove, 83, 142

Treatment
 contract, 145–47
 determining treatment needs, 122–
  25
 referral sources, listing of, 218–19
 structured intervention, 164–87
Treatment needs
 and degree of denial, 123
 and self-control, 123
 and willingness to cooperate, 123–
  24
Treatment options
 and availability of treatment, 126–
  27
 chemical dependency units, 125
 cost factors, 128
 in-patient facilities, 125, 126
 and nature of home environment,
  127
 out-patient facilities, 125
 quality of program, 129–30
 questions in decision-making
  about, 130–31
 self-help groups, 125
 therapeutic communities, 125
 and transitional nature of
  adolescence, 127–28
Treatment plan, 147
 and cooperation of teen, 158–63

Uppers, 67

Valium, 71
Voranil, 67

Washton, Dr. Arnold, 69
Withdrawal
 and death, 122
 symptoms of, 122